RICE & SPICE

OTHER BOOKS BY ROBIN ROBERTSON

The Sacred Kitchen (with Jon Robertson)

The Vegetarian Chili Cookbook

Some Like It Hot

The Soy Gourmet

366 Simply Delicious Dairy-Free Recipes

366 Healthful Ways to Cook Tofu and Other Meat Alternatives

RICE & SPICE

100 VEGETARIAN ONE-DISH DINNERS MADE WITH THE WORLD'S MOST VERSATILE GRAIN

Robin Robertson

ILLUSTRATIONS BY BROOKE SCUDDER

THE HARVARD COMMON PRESS
BOSTON, MASSACHUSETTS

The Harvard Common Press
535 Albany Street
Boston, Massachusetts 02118

www.harvardcommonpress.com

Printed in the United States of America

Printed on acid-free paper

Library of Congress Cataloging-in-Publication Data

Robertson, Robin (Robin G.)
Rice and spice : 100 vegetarian one-dish dinners made with the
world's most versatile grain / Robin Robertson.
p. cm.
Includes bibliographical references and index.
ISBN 1-55832-159-4 (cloth : alk. paper) — ISBN 1-55832-160-8 (pbk. : alk. paper)
1. Cookery (Rice) 2. Vegetarian cookery. 3. Entrées (Cookery) I. Title.

TX809.R5 R627 2000

641.6'318—dc21   99-057901

Cover photograph by Rita Maas
Cover design by Suzanne Noli
Text design by Barbara M. Bachman
Illustrations by Brooke Scudder

10 9 8 7 6 5 4 3 2 1

This book is dedicated to

John Robbins, for being

an inspiration and a light

CONTENTS

ACKNOWLEDGMENTS

I wish to acknowledge the talented chefs who have shared their rice specialties with me over the years, especially Bill Stacks, who first taught me how to cook perfect rice. Special thanks to my husband, Jon Robertson, for his assistance and support, and to my tasters, testers, and friends Samantha Ragan, Lochlain Lewis, Gloria Siegel, John Mein, B. J. Atkinson, and Pat Davis. I also want to thank Arielle Eckstut and Dan Rosenberg for encouraging me in this project, and the staff at The Harvard Common Press.

INTRODUCTION

The simple flavor of a steaming bowl of white rice can be delicious on its own. But add some spices, a sauce, or other ingredients to tantalize the taste buds, and that simple bowl of rice can become a transporting experience. Combined with savory companions, rice readily complements the flavors surrounding it to create meals of unlimited variety. The taste and aroma of global seasonings can even evoke exotic images.

Throughout the world, from village huts to four-star restaurants, one can find transcendent rice dishes, prepared to perfection, punctuated by a wide choice of seasonings. The perfect rice dish can just as easily be the fluffy white rice of a favorite Chinese restaurant crowned with Szechwan string beans or freshly cooked basmati topped with a pungent vegetable vindaloo created in your own kitchen.

Just try choosing between the toothsome creaminess of a silky risotto and the haunting fragrance of jasmine rice steaming up through a fiery Thai curry. Or between a fruity Middle Eastern pilaf and a bowl of lusty jambalaya. And then there are times when even the best savory dish can't live up to the comforting memory of Mom's rice pudding, christened with cinnamon.

What constitutes a perfect dish of rice varies with each rice tradition, in every country where rice is eaten, for each variety of rice has its own flavor and textural characteristics. Whether I am savoring a rich curry-topped basmati spiced with cloves and cinnamon, marveling at the simplicity of a bowl of Japanese sticky rice scattered with jewel-like vegetables, or scooping up the last morsel of rice drenched with a robust Moroccan tagine, I find that I adore rice—but this has not always been so.

When I was growing up in the 1950s, rice made infrequent appearances on our dinner table. In that post–World War II era, few families strayed from the American diet pattern of meat, potatoes, and a token vegetable side dish. In my Italian-American household, pasta would replace the meat and potatoes at least twice a week, but rice was a stranger. On those rare occasions when we did have rice, it was a less than memorable side dish. My mother was a fabulous cook, but her rice, like that of countless other home cooks at the time, could be sticky, gummy, and flavorless.

The fact is, America's relationship with rice is still in the courtship stage. We are only learning now what much of the rest of the world has known about rice for thousands of years.

Rice Around the World

Rice features prominently in the cuisines of the world, from the Caribbean Islands to India, Europe, and Asia to the American South and Southwest. There are more than one hundred thousand different varieties of rice. It is grown throughout Asia, as well as in countries as diverse as Brazil, Italy, and the United States.

The United States, though, grows only two percent of the world's harvest. Over ninety percent of the world's rice grows in Asia, predominantly in China, India, Bangladesh, and Indonesia, along with Vietnam, Japan, and Pakistan. In the hot climates of Southeast Asia, rice is still cultivated on the flooded terraces called paddy fields, usually using primitive methods such as the hoe or buffalo-drawn plough.

In Asia, where rice is often eaten for breakfast, lunch, dinner, and dessert, it is also used to make milk, flour, wine, vinegar, and other products such as paper and candy. Unlike many other cereal crops, ninety-five percent of the rice produced in the world is eaten by humans, rather than livestock.

Though rice is often thought to have its origins in China, it's more likely that rice reached the marshlands of China from India over five thousand years ago with the help of birds, winds, and the sea, but China quickly became the world's leading rice producer. In China, as in many Asian countries, rice is the focal point of the meal, with other foods served as accompaniments. In fact, in China, rice is synonymous with sustenance to the extent that the phrase "I lost my rice bowl" means "I lost my job." Rice is so much a part of the culture that the translation for the Chinese greeting equivalent to "How are you?" is "Have you had your rice today?"

Rice has been a powerful symbol of life throughout the ages. A Sanskrit term for rice means "sustainer of the human race." In ancient cultures, rice was viewed as a gift of heaven, believed to have grown of its own accord to keep the granaries filled, and rice is still an important part of sacred traditions in many parts of Asia. In the Japanese Shinto religion, food offerings consisting mainly of rice are presented to the kami, or deity, as a form of worship. The same is true in Indonesia, where small woven baskets mounded with rice are found everywhere as offerings to the gods. Rice is also symbolic of knowledge and enlightenment. And the bounty of rice symbolizes happiness and abundance; hence handfuls of rice are traditionally thrown at weddings in many countries throughout the world, including the United States.

Although rice has been a part of Asian culture since 3000 B.C., it wasn't until medieval times that rice became known in Europe, when it was introduced by the Moors; it was originally thought to be a spice. Even in the 1700s, England's primary use for rice was in sweet puddings. Centuries earlier, rice had made its way throughout the Middle East, Egypt, and ancient Greece and Rome, meeting with varying degrees of popularity, depending on whether or not the terrain and climate favored its growth. Spanish and Portuguese traders are said to have introduced rice to Central and South America. Some authorities believe rice was brought to the West on slave ships, while others credit explorers such as Christopher Columbus with bringing rice to the New World.

THE AMERICAN TABLE

Colonial Americans first experimented with rice cultivation in South Carolina in 1685, but it wasn't until the mid-eighteenth century that

Southern planters succeeded in turning rice into a major export crop. The Civil War, however, ended rice cultivation in the Carolinas, and rice growing was transplanted to Louisiana, Texas, and other states, including California. Until recently, people in the United States consumed only long-grain white rice of the type grown in the American South. These days, however, more and more Americans are exploring the world's nearly limitless rice pantry.

The first packaged rice, River Brand, was introduced in the early 1900s. Boxes of "converted rice," with the comforting smile of Uncle Ben, appeared on market shelves after World War II, and quick-cooking Minute Rice was introduced in 1950. In 1961, Rice-a-Roni made its debut and almost immediately became popular. This flavorful combination of rice, pasta, and seasonings could be considered the first American pilaf. It certainly got Americans to eat more rice—during its first year, the "San Francisco treat" grossed $100 million in sales. Throughout the next decade or so, the refined white Carolina-type rice remained the norm. During the 1960s and '70s, the nutritionally superior brown rice became the darling of the natural food set. More recently, as our tastes have become more eclectic, more exotic varieties such as basmati and jasmine have gained a foothold. As we usher in the 2000s, rice is coming into its own as a staple on the American dinner table. The pasta craze of the 1980s led into a romance with rice during the '90s, and "fast" rice shops are springing up in major cities across the United States. In fact, Americans are eating twice as much rice as they were just twenty years ago—close to twenty-five pounds per person annually!

RICE FOR THE HEALTH OF IT

The world's most popular grain is gaining favor in the United States both because of a growing interest in ethnic cuisines that feature rice as a main event rather than a side dish and because of an increased awareness of diet and health, resulting in a shift away from meat as the focal point of a meal. More and more Americans are visiting ethnic restaurants and experimenting with rice-based cuisines at home.

Health-conscious people want more ways to enjoy whole grains, and rice, paired with other healthful ingredients, can meet that demand. Rice is easy to digest, it contains no cholesterol or saturated fat, and is rich in vitamins and minerals, making it a natural choice for healthier eating.

A half-cup serving of white rice contains only 82 calories (89 calories for brown) and is loaded with B-vitamins, including thiamin and niacin, iron, calcium, and other nutrients. Rice that is polished and thereby stripped of many of these vitamins and minerals is usually enriched to replace the lost nutrients.

The new USDA Food Guide Pyramid features grains prominently as the most important component of a healthful diet, suggesting six to eleven half-cup servings per day. Because rice is a rich source of complex carbohydrates, protein, fiber, vitamins, and minerals, it is an important mainstay of a vegetarian diet. When paired with beans and vegetables, rice makes a well-balanced, economical meal. But even those who have not adopted a vegetarian diet are looking for ways to go meatless at least a couple of times a week in the interest of good health, especially since a low-fat, high-fiber diet has been shown to reduce the risk of heart disease and some cancers.

Although rice lacks some of the essential amino acids to make a complete protein, its protein is stored in the body and then combines with other proteins from beans, nuts, or seeds to form a complete protein. Contrary to earlier assumptions, these foods do not need to be eaten at the same meal. However, many traditional dishes are composed of rice and beans in some form.

THE WAY TO PERFECT RICE

When I worked in restaurants during the 1980s, I cooked at least five gallons of rice every day. It had to be perfect, and it had to be ready to serve at a moment's notice with various menu items. My favorite way to cook it was to bake it in a huge stainless steel pan with vegetable stock and turmeric, producing flavorful yellow rice. It tasted great, looked beautiful on the plate, and didn't require any special attention, though I learned that timing and the rice-to-water ratio were important elements in perfect rice—the very elements that have intimidated generations of American home cooks. When not baking the rice du jour, I would often boil rice in lots of water, the same way pasta is cooked. The rice-to-water ratio was not an issue, and I could test it periodically while prepping other ingredients for the evening's menu. It worked like a charm.

Over the years, I have come to think of rice as a reliable convenience food. When I have cooked rice on hand, I can get a healthful meal on the table in minutes. Rice cooked in advance provides a culinary opportunity for great taste and nutrition, as it can form the basis of a vast number of vegetarian entrées that are easy to make and quick to serve. Whether stir-fried, steamed, baked, or boiled, rice dishes can provide well-balanced and inexpensive main-course meals in minutes. And some rice varieties cook in less than twenty minutes, allowing even fresh-cooked rice meals to be ready in less than a half hour.

Within these pages, you will discover a wide variety of rice dishes and preparations, using many seasonings from the global spice rack, along with vegetables, beans, and sauces. These 100 quick-and-easy vegetarian recipes highlight the subtle variations in taste and texture among rice varieties— such as basmati, jasmine, brown, and arborio—combined with fresh ingredients and flavorful spices in an enticing array of international delights.

Rice and Spice is for busy people who are short on time but want to eat well and prepare versatile, flavorful, and healthful vegetarian entrées for their families and friends. There are recipes for all tastes and all occasions. Since one of my goals was to show how rice can be used as a convenience food, a majority of the recipes call for precooked rice.

The first chapter covers basic rice cooking techniques and provides useful information, such as storage and preparation guidelines. Chapters Two and Three are devoted to recipes from China, Japan, and Korea, as well as Thailand, India, and other Asian countries where rice is a way of life and rice cooking an art.

Chapter Four explores other rice-savvy cuisines of the world, including those of the Middle East, Italy, and Spain. Chapter Five is dedicated to American rice dishes, including both classics and tempting new innovations.

These five international chapters include recipes for delectable stir-fries, pilafs, and risottos, as well as rich sauces and other tasty toppings to spoon over rice. Following these are one chapter each devoted to hearty soups and main-dish salads that feature rice as a main ingredient. Finally, since no rice cookbook would be complete without an homage to the venerable rice pudding, *Rice and Spice* ends on a sweet note with a chapter of rice desserts.

By the time you've explored these pages and experimented with the recipes, you will be convinced of the versatility of rice. And, as more of us discover the pleasures of rice, we may find that the "meat and potatoes" era has been replaced with a "rice and vegetables" sensibility.

"Have you had your rice today?"

Rice & Spice

CHAPTER 1

Making Perfect Rice

Learning how to prepare rice perfectly will open the door to a world of international rice cooking that will enhance your culinary versatility and expand your mealtime options. This chapter provides the basics of rice cooking, as well as specific ways to make rice convenient and easy to use. If you have rarely ventured beyond everyday white rice, you are in for a new experience. Even if you are already familiar with the seductive aroma of jasmine rice or the chewy texture of short-grain brown rice, there are still plenty of delicious discoveries ahead.

The first step is to discover the diversity, subtle taste, and textural nuances of the different rice varieties. There are a lot of choices out there: Pick your favorites, but try new ones too. For the most authentic dining experience when preparing an ethnic meal, choose a type of rice that is traditional to that cuisine. However, the creative cook will also want to experiment with rice in unexpected combinations, moving beyond the suggestions provided in this book. For example, pair Indian basmati with a French sauté. Enhance the aromatic quality of Thai jasmine with the tangy sweetness of American barbecued beans or Caribbean jerk-spiced vegetables.

One of the most endearing qualities of rice is that it takes on the flavors around it, allowing for seemingly limitless variations on a basic rice recipe. Whether seasoned with toasted sesame oil, tamari, or grated ginger or enlivened with lemon zest or fresh herbs, rice easily adapts to most any ethnic flavor nuance that comes its way.

A simple way to transform any rice into a welcome convenience food is to cook a quantity in advance for later use. This is also especially handy when you want to make a fried rice recipe, since these call for cold cooked rice. For other recipes, rice can be easily reheated without compromising its taste or texture (see "Reheating Rice," page 15). On the other hand, some varieties of rice cook in only 15 minutes—less than some types of pasta. And, unlike pasta, rice can be kept warm for up to 30 minutes after cooking and still retain its character.

A Guide to Rice

Along with other distinguishing characteristics, rice varieties are classified based on the length of the grain: long, medium, and short—although in most countries, just short- and long-grain are used. The grain length affects how it cooks, with long-grain rice cooking up as fluffy, separate grains and short-grain rice having a tendency to clump together. Medium-grain rice falls somewhere in between.

- **Short-grain rice:** These almost-round grains are nearly as wide as they are long. They tend to stick together when cooked, because of their high starch content, and are good used in puddings or soups. Examples of short-grain rice are the Japanese sticky rice that is used to make sushi and the arborio rice of Italy that is the basis for risotto.
- **Medium-grain rice:** With slightly longer grains than short-grain rice and a moderate starch content, medium-grain rice often overlaps both long- and short-grain rice in its uses. Valencia rice from Spain is the medium-grain rice that is used to make paella.
- **Long-grain rice:** These slender grains remain separate when cooked and are the most popular type of rice. Long-grain rice has the least starch and is favored in a multitude of savory dishes because of its fluffy texture.

In addition to being classified by size, rice can be described by color. The most common color is white, which means that the rice has been "polished," or milled, to remove the outer coating, known as the bran. In the United

States, most white rice is enriched with iron, niacin, and thiamin to compensate for the loss of vitamins and minerals removed with the nutritious outer layer.

The natural bran layer has been left intact in brown rice, thus accounting for its color. As such, brown rice is more nutritious than white rice. It is chewy, with a mildly nutty flavor, and takes longer to cook than white rice. Its nutritional value makes brown rice popular in the health food market, where organic varieties are often sought.

The term *organic rice* can refer to any variety of rice that has been grown without the use of pesticides or synthetic fertilizer. Like other organic foods, it is more expensive than its nonorganically grown counterparts.

Black rice is actually a brown rice with a dark hull. It is grown in China, Thailand, and Bali, as well as California. Black rice varieties can be found in specialty food shops or as part of rice blends.

The staple rice of Bhutan is a red rice that turns pink when cooked. In general, red rice is not as popular as black rice and other exotics. One notable exception is the French Camarguais red rice.

Another classification of rice has to do with processing. Supermarket shelves contain a selection of rices with such labels as "parboiled" or "instant." Parboiling is an ancient method of processing rice before milling. It originated between two and four thousand years ago in southern India, and parboiled rice is still the preferred rice for many people there, as well as in Bangladesh, Sri Lanka, and Bengal. Parboiled rice is also a popular product in Europe, Australia, and the United States. The parboiling process actually steams the rice under pressure, which helps retain some of the nutrients that would otherwise then be lost in the milling process. However, many people feel this process produces rice with less flavor. In the United States, parboiled rice is usually packaged with specific cooking instructions, Uncle Ben's Converted Rice being the most widely known.

Instant rice is precooked, dehydrated, and then cooked again, resulting in a loss of flavor and texture. And it still takes 10 minutes to cook—only a few minutes less than many raw varieties.

Even supermarkets now carry a varied selection of rice options that were once only available at specialty food shops. Most rice eaten in the world belongs to the Asian variety *Oryza sativa,* which is divided into two main groups: indica and japonica. There is also a third smaller group called javanica. Indica rice is usually long-grain and grows better in hot climates; basmati and Carolina-type long-grain rice are two examples. Japonica rice is usually medium- to short-grain and is best grown in temperate climates. Examples include Japanese rice and rice varieties of the Mediterranean.

Here is a guide to both the most common varieties of rice available, and some of the more exotic types:

- **Arborio** is a short-grain Italian rice known for making creamy risottos. Its soft, creamy texture also makes it a good choice for puddings and other rice desserts. Other premium Italian rices used for risotto are carnaroli and vialone nano.
- **Basmati** is a fragrant long-grain rice from India, where its name means "queen of fragrance." Interestingly, when basmati rice is cooked, the grains become longer but not wider, and they remain separate and fluffy.
- **Black rice** is an exotic rice with a black (rather than brown) bran layer. Like other unmilled rices, it needs to cook in more water and for a longer period of time than polished rice. It is grown in California as well as Asian countries.
- **Brown rice** (whole-grain rice) is nutritionally superior to white rice because it is unpolished, and has thus not been stripped of its nutrients. There are three types: short-, medium-, and long-grain, all of which have slightly different flavors and textures and require different cooking times. Short-grain brown rice can take up to twice as long to cook as white rice.
- **Jasmine rice**, used in Thai cooking, is an aromatic long-grain rice with a delicate flowery bouquet. When cooked, it becomes slightly sticky.
- **Pecan rice** is a long-grain rice from Louisiana named for its nutty flavor and aroma (it does not contain pecans).
- **Sticky rice,** or glutinous rice, is a short- to medium-grain rice used in many Asian dishes, especially desserts. Despite the name, glutinous rice,

like all other rices, contains no gluten. The stickiness is the result of the high starch content. Japanese-style sticky rice is used to make sushi.

- **Texmati** is a cross between basmati rice and American long-grain rice. It is grown in California by Lundberg Family Farms, a company that markets a number of exotic rice varieties to mainstream America.
- **Wehani** is a reddish-brown hybrid rice with a nutty flavor. It is grown in California by Lundberg Farms.
- **White rice** (polished rice) is rice that has had the hull, bran, and germ removed, thus stripping it of its color and nutrients. It is often enriched with vitamins and minerals to make up for their loss. It comes in short-, medium-, and long-grain varieties, with long-grain being the most popular.
- **Wild rice** is not a rice at all, but the seed of a tall aquatic grass. Once only found primarily in marshes and on riverbanks in North America, it was prized as a nutritious resource by Native Americans. Most of the "wild" rice we eat now is cultivated in irrigated fields. Though quite expensive, wild rice contains nearly twice as much protein as white rice, and it is high in amino acids and B vitamins. It is often paired with white rice to add color, taste, and texture to pilafs.

Storing Rice

Most raw rice will keep for up to a year in a tightly sealed container in a cool dry place (bay leaves can be added to the container to prevent bugs). Because of the natural oil content of its bran layer, however, brown rice should be stored in the refrigerator to prevent rancidity.

Cooked rice will keep well for up to 3 days in the refrigerator. Allow hot rice to cool completely at room temperature, then cover with a tight-fitting lid and refrigerate. If it is covered before it is cool, the rice will continue to steam and become mushy. Cooked rice can also be portioned and stored in the freezer for up to 2 weeks. To thaw, simply transfer the frozen container to the refrigerator to thaw for a few hours or, for a quick-thaw method, place in a colander under running water.

The Choice Is Yours

Despite rumors to the contrary, there is no great mystery to cooking perfect rice. There are several ways to make foolproof rice, including boiling, steaming, baking, and pressure-cooking.

Among the points to consider are whether rice should be cooked covered or uncovered, in a lot of water or in a small amount, and whether it should be stirred or left undisturbed. There are also conflicting opinions as to whether rice should be soaked prior to cooking, and what the texture of the cooked rice should be.

Texture, of course, depends primarily on the type of rice that is cooked and its intended purpose. For example, a soft, sticky quality is desirable in sushi rice; brown rice is characteristically chewy; and basmati rice is best when cooked into dry, separate grains. Often, however, it's a matter of personal taste: A good rule of thumb for most rice is a tender texture that is neither mushy nor too firm. Some people, though, prefer very soft rice, others like it more al dente.

To ensure that a satisfying rice-based meal is only minutes away, you can take a tip from restaurant kitchens and cook a large quantity of rice in advance, ready for quick meals for several days. But keep in mind that many varieties of rice cook in as little as 15 to 20 minutes. If you put on a pot of rice when you enter the kitchen to prepare dinner, it will be done by the time the rest of your meal is ready.

Following are instructions for several cooking methods and other rice preparation rituals, such as soaking and washing. Experiment to see which works best for you.

Washing Rice

Most packaged rice is quite clean and doesn't require washing. In fact, packages of enriched rice and certain others, such as arborio, bear specific instructions not to wash them. But rice that is imported or purchased in bulk may contain hulls, dust, and foreign particles and should be washed.

To wash rice, place it in a bowl of cold water and swish the water with your fingers or a spoon. Any bits of loose matter should rise to the top. You can then pour off the liquid and proceed with cooking.

Soaking Rice

The primary reason for soaking rice is to increase the moisture content, thus enabling the cooking water to penetrate the grains more easily. In most cases, soaking doesn't affect the cooking process much, although some experts feel it helps prevent the rice from sticking together. Since some moisture is absorbed when rice is washed, many people skip the soaking step with rice that has been washed; others skip it in any case. There are a few varieties of rice, however, such as sticky, or glutinous, rice, that do require soaking in order to be perfectly cooked. Some cooks also prefer to soak basmati rice to produce longer grains when cooked.

COOKING METHODS

In many cases, the preferred cooking method is determined by the variety of rice. For example, arborio rice is best when it is first sautéed and then hot liquid is slowly added as it cooks.

While certain cooking methods reflect a culture or tradition, others are determined by the characteristics of the particular rice, especially how readily it absorbs water. This is usually determined by whether the rice is waxy or nonwaxy. *Waxy* and *nonwaxy* refer to the amount of two starches, amylose and amylopectin, in a rice. Waxy rice tends to have low amylose levels and higher amylopectin levels. Examples of waxy rices are sticky (or glutinous) varieties, such as Japanese rice, or Thai jasmine. Nonwaxy rice, on the other hand, is high in amylose, with low levels of amylopectin. Basmati and most long-grain rices fall into this category. In general, waxy low-amylose rices tend to absorb less water when cooked and nonwaxy high-amylose rices absorb more water and expand more during the cooking process. Nonwaxy rice cooks up drier and fluffier, while waxy rice is sticky and clings together.

Even so, most rice varieties can be cooked using the same methods, with various adjustments in cooking time and/or water to rice ratios.

These basic recipes serve as the foundations for most of the recipes in this book. Unless otherwise indicated, the proportions given in the recipes are for long-grain white rice. Here are some tips to keep in mind:

- Rice is most commonly cooked in salted water, but you can use vegetable stock or add a vegetable bouillon cube for extra flavor.
- Some cooks like to add up to a tablespoon of oil or butter to the cooking water, in the belief that it keeps the rice from sticking together; it is not necessary.
- The easiest way to test rice for doneness is to scoop a few grains from the pot and bite into them. They should be tender but still firm, with no hardness in the center.
- For a dry variety like basmati, or for very soft rice, use up to ¼ cup additional water.
- Brown rice may need up to an additional ½ cup water and will generally need to cook up to 15 minutes longer than white rice.
- If rice is to be used for fried rice, use slightly less cooking water to achieve a drier fluffier rice.
- On the average, rice nearly triples in bulk when cooked, although yields vary with particular rice varieties. For example, 2 cups of jasmine may yield 4½ to 5 cups of cooked rice, but the same amount of basmati may result in up to 6 cups of cooked rice.
- Cooking rice in a pot that's too small could be one reason your rice turns out less than perfect. Raw rice should be no more than 1½ to 2 inches deep in the pot. Try the old-fashioned "knuckle test": Touch the bottom of the pot with your index finger—the raw rice should not come up past the second joint of your finger.

In countries where rice is the main focus of the meal and other dishes are meant to complement it, one person can easily eat 2 to 3 cups of rice at one sitting. To those who think of rice as a side dish, on the other hand, 1 cup would seem like a large portion.

In this book, one serving is 1 to 2 cups rice, depending on the recipe. For example, when a simple rice dish is a main course, 2 cups is a generous portion; if the rice is combined with a number of other ingredients, 1 to 1½ cups would be more reasonable. Most soups and desserts call for a cup or less of rice per serving. Since most of the recipes in this book are for main-course meals, as in those countries where rice is exalted, the "more is better" philosophy is advised.

If you're like many of us, as you become more enamored of rice-based cuisines, you may find you need to start making more rice for each meal. In my house, there are rarely leftovers. To be sure of them, I need to plan to make extra rice to store for later use. But, given the number of exciting recipes in the book that call for precooked rice, ending up with a large quantity of leftover rice is an ideal to strive for.

In other words, if you'll need 4 cups of cooked rice for tonight's curry dinner, make 6 or 8 cups. That way, you'll be halfway to preparing tomorrow night's Thai Fried Rice.

RICE COOKING CHART

The following chart gives cooking times and water amounts for the most common types of rice using the absorption (steaming) method. (On the average, 2 cups of raw rice will yield approximately 5 to 6 cups of cooked rice.) Soaking, altitude, and age of the grain may all influence the outcome, so be sure to monitor the rice as it cooks and test for doneness.

In each case, the pot should be removed from heat at end of cooking time and allowed to rest for 5 minutes.

NOTE: For mixed rice blends, parboiled rice, and instant rice, follow the cooking directions on the package.

RICE (2 CUPS)	WATER / CUPS	COOKING TIME
BASMATI RICE	3¾ TO 4 CUPS	18 TO 20 MINUTES
BLACK RICE	4½ CUPS	30 MINUTES
JASMINE RICE	3½ CUPS	15 MINUTES
LONG-GRAIN BROWN RICE	4 CUPS	30 MINUTES
LONG-GRAIN WHITE RICE	4 CUPS	18 TO 20 MINUTES
RED RICE	4¼ CUPS	35 TO 40 MINUTES
SHORT-GRAIN BROWN RICE	4¾ TO 5 CUPS	45 TO 50 MINUTES
STICKY (GLUTINOUS) RICE	3 CUPS	15 TO 20 MINUTES
WILD RICE	5 CUPS	40 TO 50 MINUTES

STEAMED RICE

STEAMING, also called the absorption method, is the most common method of cooking rice. It is done by cooking rice in a precise amount of water in a covered saucepan on top of the stove.

2 cups long-grain white rice
4 cups water
½ teaspoon salt

Place the rice, water, and salt in a medium saucepan and bring to a boil over medium heat. Reduce the heat, cover with a tight-fitting lid, and cook over very low heat for 20 minutes, or until the rice is tender. Remove from the heat and let rest for 5 minutes with the lid on. Fluff with a fork before serving.

MAKES 6 CUPS

BOILED RICE

COOKING rice in a large amount of water, like pasta, makes precise measurements unnecessary, but some of the nutrients get washed away when the rice is drained.

8 to 10 cups water
¾ teaspoon salt
2 cups long-grain white rice

Bring the water and salt to a rapid boil in a large pot over high heat. Add the rice, reduce the heat to medium, and simmer uncovered. Start testing the rice for doneness at about 15 minutes. When it is tender, drain in a colander.

MAKES 6 CUPS

Baked Rice

THIS method is especially useful when you are using the oven for another dish, or when all of the stove burners are spoken for. (Another plus is that you can cook and serve it in the same dish.) Baked rice cooks up light and fluffy.

2 cups long-grain white rice
¾ teaspoon salt (or 1 vegetable bouillon cube or
1 teaspoon granules dissolved in
¼ cup of the boiling water)
1 teaspoon olive oil
3¾ cups boiling water

Preheat the oven to 350°F. In a lightly oiled 2½-quart casserole dish, combine the rice, salt (or dissolved bouillon), and oil. Add the boiling water and cover with lightly oiled parchment paper cut to fit inside the rim of the dish, and then with aluminum foil or a tight-fitting lid. Bake for 25 to 30 minutes, or until the rice is tender. Remove from the oven and let the rice rest for 5 minutes. Fluff with a fork and serve.

MAKES 6 CUPS

Pressure-Cooked Rice

USED primarily for short-grain brown rice and other longer-cooking rices, such as black, red, or wild, pressure-cooking needs less water than other methods because there is less evaporation during the cooking process. The texture of pressure-cooked rice is usually softer than steamed or boiled rice.

1½ cups short-grain brown rice
3 cups water
½ teaspoon salt

Combine the rice, water, and salt in a pressure cooker and bring up to full pressure over medium-high heat. Reduce the heat to low and cook for 30 minutes. Remove the pressure cooker from the heat and let stand for 10 minutes. Release the pressure, using the quick-release method, remove the lid, and fluff the rice with a fork.

MAKES ABOUT 5 CUPS

MICROWAVED RICE

COOKING in a microwave oven doesn't save any time; the main advantage to microwaving rice is that you don't need to put a large pot on the stove. You can cook and serve it in the same container, and, in the summertime, an added benefit is that cooking the rice does not heat up the kitchen.

2 cups long-grain white rice
3¾ cups water
½ teaspoon salt

Place the rice, water and salt in a microwave-safe container. Cover with a lid, plastic wrap, or a plate and cook for 15 minutes on high power. Check for doneness, then microwave for another 5 to 10 minutes if necessary, or until tender. Let stand for 5 minutes, then fluff the rice with a fork.

MAKES 6 CUPS

STEAMED STICKY (GLUTINOUS) RICE

STICKY, or glutinous, rice should be soaked in water prior to cooking for a minimum of 1 hour, preferably up to 8 hours, or overnight. In most Asian countries, sticky rice is sweetened and served as a dessert. Notable exceptions include Japan and the highlands of Vietnam, where sticky rice is the rice of choice at mealtimes. Sticky rice is traditionally made in a steamer, often wrapped in cheesecloth before being placed in the steamer basket.

1 ½ cups sticky (glutinous) rice
Water

Place the rice in a bowl with enough cold water to cover it completely. Soak for at least 1 hour, or overnight. Drain the rice and place in the center of a steamer basket that has been lined with a piece of moist cheesecloth. Set over rapidly boiling water, cover tightly with a lid, and steam for about 20 minutes, or until the rice is tender. Let stand for 5 to 10 minutes before serving.

MAKES 4 ½ CUPS

NOTE: To prepare sticky rice by the absorption method, combine 2 cups (soaked) rice with 2½ cups water. Cover and simmer for 15 minutes, or until tender, remove from the heat, and let stand for 10 minutes.

PILAF-STYLE RICE

ONE of the classic ways to prepare rice is pilaf-style: Raw rice is sautéed in oil or butter with onions and other seasonings, until the grains are coated, then water is added, the pan is covered, and the rice is cooked by the absorption method until done.

ELECTRIC RICE STEAMER

CONVENIENT and easy to use, the electric rice steamer is a boon to rice lovers everywhere. When the rice is cooked, the steamer shuts off automatically, then switches itself on and off at intervals to keep the rice hot until needed. To use a rice steamer, follow the instructions that come with your particular cooker, but be sure not to add salt, since it can corrode the appliance.

REHEATING RICE

Cooked rice can be a lifesaver when you need to prepare a meal in a hurry. Cold cooked rice can be reheated in a number of ways:

- **Steam:** Put the cooked rice in a colander over a pan of lightly boiling water. Cover and steam until heated through, being careful not to leave on the heat too long, or the rice will become mushy.
- **Stovetop:** Add cooked rice to a saucepan with 2 tablespoons water, cover, and cook over medium-low heat for 3 to 5 minutes, or until hot, stirring occasionally with a fork.
- **Bake:** Put the cooked rice in a lightly oiled casserole dish, add about 2 tablespoons hot water, cover tightly, and bake in a preheated 375°F oven for 20 minutes, or until hot.
- **Microwave:** Place the cooked rice in a microwave-safe container, add 2 tablespoons hot water, cover, and microwave for 2 minutes, or until hot.

OTHER INGREDIENTS

So much about cooking is a personal choice. Just as I encourage you to explore the world of rice varieties and cook creatively, so, too, do I believe there are no hard-and-fast rules about certain other ingredients. As a vegetarian, of course, I use no meat products. In these recipes, I also suggest alternative choices to dairy products wherever possible. Like most health-conscious people, I believe that fresh organic ingredients are best and I avoid highly processed food. I recommend sea salt over regular table salt and would encourage readers to try natural sweeteners in favor of sugar (see Note, page 133). I prefer tamari sauce to regular soy sauce because of the additives many brands of soy sauce contain. However, if you can find a good soy sauce that is reasonably pure, then by all means use it.

Regarding cooking oils, while I suggest olive oil (extra virgin) and sesame oil (dark or toasted) for flavor in certain dishes, I leave the choice of vegetable oil up to the individual. In general, choose a good-quality, cold-pressed oil. Some people prefer peanut oil for stir-frying because it does well at high temperatures; others use safflower oil because it is low in saturated fat. Some swear by canola oil, others only use corn oil.

Throughout the book, when using beans, I call for cooked beans. While many purists prefer to cook dried beans from scratch, for sheer convenience, you can't beat canned beans. Beans are one of the few canned products that retain good texture and flavor. Canned organic brands are best for overall quality, as well as because of their lower sodium content. Although can sizes vary, 15- and 16-ounce cans, which contain about 1½ cups beans, are the most common. Be sure to rinse any canned beans before using.

The Perfect Complement

Rice and beans are a natural combination, and in many countries, favorite dishes combine rice with beans or bean products such as tofu. In turn, many of the recipes in this book follow suit. Besides being a perfect complement in taste and texture, rice and beans, eaten together, increase the number of amino acids delivered to the body and maximize the available protein. Beans and grains do not have to be eaten at the same time in order to combine properly in the body, as was once believed. In recent years, it has been discovered that since the body digests proteins more slowly than once thought, the amino acids taken in at one meal are still available to combine with others ingested later in the day.

With so many delicious ways to savor rice and beans in the same dish, though, why not continue the tradition? Still, for those of us following a vegetarian diet, it's good to know that, should we choose, we can enjoy these foods at different times or in combination with other ingredients and still reap the same benefits.

RICETERA...
SPICING UP RICE

SINCE RICE readily takes on surrounding flavors, you can easily transform basic rice into a dazzling taste sensation with one of these simple additions:

- Citrus zest—Add grated lemon, lime, or orange zest to cooked rice for a lively fresh taste.
- Coconut milk— Replace 1 cup or more of the cooking water with unsweetened coconut milk for a tropical flavor. This adds a special flair to rice for Southeast Asian dishes or desserts.
- Curry powder—Heat in a small amount of vegetable oil, stirring until fragrant, then add cooked rice, along with some raisins and a bit of chutney, for a quick taste of India.
- Fresh herbs—Toss hot cooked rice with your choice of minced fresh herbs to enhance flavor and color.
- Indian spices—Heat 4 whole cloves, 2 cardamom pods, 1 cinnamon stick, and 1 bay leaf in 1 teaspoon oil, stirring over medium heat, until fragrant, then add to rice as it cooks. Remove the spices just prior to serving.
- Nuts—Stir chopped lightly toasted nuts into cooked rice for added flavor and crunch.
- Pesto—Gently stir a generous amount of pesto sauce into hot cooked rice.
- Saffron—Use this expensive spice sparingly to add a golden color and distinct flavor to rice dishes (it is traditionally used in bouillabaisse, paella, and risotto Milanese).
- Tamari—Add tamari sauce instead of salt to the cooking water to impart flavor and imbue the rice with a rich brown color.
- Turmeric—Add to the cooking water to transform rice into a bright yellow color (an economical alternative to saffron).

CHAPTER 2

East Asian Inspiration

In light of the long and cherished history of rice in East Asian countries, it is fitting that we begin with recipes inspired by the cuisines of China, Japan, and Korea. In these countries, rice is the main part of the meal, and the quick preparation of delicious meals is an art. Often rice is eaten at all three meals each day. While the people of most Asian countries eat long-grain white rice, the Japanese prefer their sticky rice.

Many of the recipes in this section, such as Green Beans and Rice with Sesame-Orange Sauce, are for stir-fries, the quick Asian cooking method that retains the vital nutrients of the fresh ingredients that are served over rice. Others, like Vegetable Donburi and Congee, are East Asian comfort food at its best. Soy sauce is an almost universal condiment in Asia, although each country has its own indigenous spices and other ingredients that help to make its cuisine distinctive.

Spicy Tofu and Broccoli Stir-Fry

ಌ Bright green broccoli flowerets spiced with a garlicky ginger sauce provide a striking contrast to tofu and snowy white rice.

¼ cup tamari or other soy sauce

2 tablespoons water

1 teaspoon sugar (or a natural sweetener to taste)

¼ teaspoon salt

1 tablespoon dark sesame oil

2 teaspoons cornstarch

1 tablespoon vegetable oil

4 cups broccoli flowerets

1 tablespoon minced garlic

1 tablespoon minced fresh ginger

1 teaspoon hot red pepper flakes

8 ounces firm tofu, drained, blotted dry, and cut into ½-inch cubes

3 tablespoons minced scallions

4 to 6 cups hot cooked long-grain white rice

In a small bowl, stir together the tamari, water, sugar, salt, sesame oil, and cornstarch. Set aside. In a large skillet or wok, heat the vegetable oil over medium-high heat until hot. Add the broccoli and stir-fry for 30 seconds, or until bright green. With a slotted spoon, transfer to paper towels to drain. Add the garlic, ginger, red pepper flakes, and tofu to the pan and stir-fry for 30 seconds. Return the broccoli to the pan and stir-fry for 1 minute. Add the tamari mixture and the scallions and stir-fry for 1 minute, or until the broccoli is well coated with the sauce. Serve over the rice.

SERVES 4 TO 6

Green Beans and Rice with Sesame-Orange Sauce

 ✺ Although long-grain white rice would be traditional in this Chinese-inspired dish, you might try jasmine or basmati to complement the sweetness of the orange sauce. Asian chile paste is available in Asian grocery stores and well-stocked supermarkets.

¾ cup fresh orange juice
1 tablespoon Asian chile paste, or to taste
1 tablespoon light brown sugar
1 tablespoon tamari or other soy sauce
1 tablespoon fresh lemon juice
1 tablespoon dark sesame oil
2 teaspoons vegetable oil
2 garlic cloves, minced
1 pound green beans, trimmed and halved diagonally
¼ cup minced onion
½ cup water
1 tablespoon arrowroot, dissolved in 1 tablespoon water
4 to 6 cups hot cooked long-grain white rice
1 tablespoon toasted sesame seeds, for garnish

In a small bowl, combine the orange juice, chile paste, brown sugar, tamari, lemon juice, and sesame oil; set aside. Heat the vegetable oil in a large skillet or wok over medium heat until hot. Add the garlic, green beans, and onion and stir-fry for 2 minutes, then add the water, cover, and steam until the vegetables are tender, about 3 to 4 minutes. Pour in the sesame-orange sauce, stir, and cook until hot, about 2 minutes. Stir in the arrowroot mixture and continue to cook for 1 minute, or until the sauce comes to a boil and thickens. Serve immediately over the rice, garnished with the toasted sesame seeds.

SERVES 4

HOISIN-GLAZED TOFU
OVER RICE

H O I S I N sauce, a flavorful Chinese condiment similar to barbecue sauce, adds an exotic sweet spiciness to any stir-fry. It can be found in Asian markets and well-stocked supermarkets. I like the taste and textural effect achieved by combining half white and half brown rice, but any rice would be great in this recipe.

1 pound extra-firm tofu, drained and blotted dry
¼ cup hoisin sauce
2 tablespoons tamari or other soy sauce
2 tablespoons water
1 tablespoon vegetable oil
1 tablespoon minced fresh ginger
2 tablespoons minced scallions
¼ teaspoon hot red pepper flakes
2 ½ cups cooked long-grain white rice
2 ½ cups cooked long-grain brown rice
1 tablespoon dark sesame oil

Cut the tofu into ½-inch-wide slices and set aside. In a small bowl, combine the hoisin, tamari, and water; set aside. Heat the oil in a large skillet or wok over medium heat until hot. Add the ginger, scallions, and red pepper flakes and stir-fry for about 10 seconds, or until fragrant. Add the hoisin mixture and bring to a simmer, stirring. Add the tofu and stir until heated through, about 2 minutes. Meanwhile, in a large skillet or saucepan, heat both rices together with the sesame oil, tossing to coat. Serve the tofu over the rice.

SERVES 4

Bok Choy and
Shiitake Stir-Fry

〜〜 BOK CHOY, a type of Chinese cabbage, is a common ingredient in Chinese stir-fries. It has a subtle, slightly sweet flavor that is milder than regular cabbage. Tofu chunks can be added to this stir-fry to boost the protein content.

1 tablespoon vegetable oil

2 garlic cloves, minced

1 tablespoon minced fresh ginger

1 small onion, thinly sliced

1 small hot chile, seeded and minced

8 ounces shiitake mushrooms, stemmed and sliced

3 tablespoons tamari or other soy sauce

½ cup water

1 tablespoon dry sherry

½ teaspoon sugar

1 bunch bok choy, cut crosswise into ½-inch strips

1 tablespoon cornstarch, dissolved in 1 tablespoon water

4 to 6 cups hot cooked long-grain white or brown rice

Heat the oil in a large skillet or wok over medium-high heat until hot. Add the garlic and ginger and stir-fry until fragrant, about 30 seconds. Add the onion, chiles, and shiitakes and stir-fry until the onion is softened, about 5 minutes. Add the tamari, water, sherry, and sugar, and stir to coat. Add the bok choy and stir-fry until wilted. Add the cornstarch mixture and continue stirring until the sauce thickens. Serve over the rice.

SERVES 4

Szechwan Tempeh over Rice

Tempeh is made of compressed fermented soybeans, which are formed into cakes, like tofu. Its meaty texture is terrific in stir-fries such as this one, where it stands up well to the assertiveness of the spicy Szechwan seasonings.

1 tablespoon vegetable oil

1 pound tempeh, cut into ½-inch-wide slices

1 carrot, cut diagonally into ¼-inch slices

1 green bell pepper, cut into 1-inch squares

1 garlic clove, minced

2 teaspoons minced fresh ginger

2 scallions, trimmed and minced

¼ teaspoon hot red pepper flakes

2 tablespoons dry sherry

2 tablespoons tamari or other soy sauce

½ cup vegetable stock or water

1 tablespoon cornstarch, dissolved in 1½ tablespoons water

4 to 6 cups hot cooked long-grain white or brown rice

Heat the oil in a large skillet or wok over medium-high heat until hot. Add the tempeh and stir-fry until golden, about 2 minutes. Add the carrot and bell pepper and stir-fry for 1 minute, or until slightly softened. Stir in the garlic, ginger, scallions, and red pepper flakes, and stir-fry for about 30 seconds, until fragrant. Stir in the sherry, tamari, and stock or water. Then stir in the cornstarch mixture and cook until the sauce thickens. Serve over the rice.

SERVES 4

CONGEE

CONGEE is a simple restorative porridge that is traditionally served at breakfast in China, but it can be enjoyed any time of the day. If you like, serve it accompanied by small bowls of chopped scallions, chopped peanuts, chile paste, and soy sauce, to be added according to personal taste.

1 cup long-grain white rice
6 cups water
½ teaspoon salt
1 small onion, minced
1 cup finely shredded Napa cabbage
1 tablespoon minced fresh ginger
1 teaspoon minced garlic
1 tablespoon tamari or other soy sauce

In a large saucepan, combine the rice, water, and salt and bring to a boil. Reduce the heat to low and add the onion, cabbage, ginger, garlic, and tamari. Cover and cook, stirring occasionally, for 45 minutes, or until thick and creamy. Serve in large soup bowls, accompanied by the condiments suggested in the headnote.

SERVES 4

VEGETABLE DONBURI

DONBURI is usually made with eggs, but for a vegetarian version, silken tofu stands in nicely. Serve in oversized rice bowls for an authentic touch. Japanese sticky rice is traditional, but any variety of rice would work well in this dish.

1 (12-ounce) block silken tofu, drained and blotted dry
1 tablespoon vegetable oil
1 large onion, finely chopped
1 carrot, grated
1 cup stemmed and thinly sliced shiitake mushrooms (about 4)
¼ cup tamari or other soy sauce
1 teaspoon sugar (or a natural sweetener to taste)
4 cups hot cooked Japanese sticky (glutinous) or other rice
1 teaspoon dark sesame oil
1 tablespoon toasted sesame seeds, for garnish

Crumble the tofu into a bowl and set aside. Heat the oil in a large skillet or wok over medium-high heat until hot. Add the onion and stir-fry until soft, about 5 minutes. Add the carrot and mushrooms and cook about 1 minute longer, until softened. Stir in the tamari, sugar, and tofu, stirring to combine, and cook until the tofu is heated through. Serve over the hot rice, drizzled with the toasted sesame oil and sprinkled with the sesame seeds.

SERVES 4

NORI MAKI   JAPANESE RICE ROLLS

෨෨ N o rice book would be complete without this Japanese mainstay. Nori maki are a type of sushi made of sticky rice and a filling rolled up in a sheet of nori seaweed and cut into bite-sized pieces. Sushi does not need to be made with raw fish, and many different vegetables make great filling choices. Nori, wasabi, pickled ginger, and bamboo sushi mats (called *sudare*) are available at Asian markets, natural food stores, and many supermarkets.

⅓ cup rice wine vinegar

1 teaspoon sugar

4 cups hot cooked Japanese sticky (glutinous) rice

6 nori sheets

2 tablespoons wasabi paste (Japanese horseradish)

4 strips carrot (slice the carrot lengthwise into strips ¼ inch thick × 4 inches
    long), blanched in boiling water for 30 seconds

4 strips cucumber (¼ inch thick × 4 inches long, sliced like the carrot)

4 thin slices avocado (¼ inch thick × 4 inches long)

Pickled ginger, for garnish

Tamari or other soy sauce, for serving

Bring the vinegar to a simmer in a small saucepan. Add the sugar and stir until dissolved. Place the hot cooked rice in a large shallow bowl and pour the vinegar mixture over it. Fan the rice until cool. Cover with a damp cloth so the rice does not dry out. Place 1 sheet of nori on a bamboo sushi mat or a clean cloth napkin. Spread ¾ cup of the rice evenly over the nori, leaving a ½-inch border at the top and bottom edges. Spread ½ teaspoon of the wasabi paste across the rice closest to you. Place 2 carrot strips end to end on top of the wasabi.

Beginning at the end nearest you, roll up the nori, using the sushi mat and pressing firmly against the nori to make a compact roll; be sure to keep the end of the sushi mat from rolling into the sushi. Wet the exposed edge of the nori with a little water, gently squeeze the mat around the sushi roll to seal, and remove the mat. Using a sharp knife, cut the sushi roll in half, then cut each half into thirds to create 6 pieces. Stand the pieces on end on a large serving platter.

Repeat with the remaining nori sheets, rice, wasabi, and carrot, then the cucumber and avocado. Garnish the sushi platter with pickled ginger. Shape the remaining 1 tablespoon wasabi into a small mound on the platter, and place a small bowl of tamari for dipping alongside.

MAKES 6 ROLLS, OR 36 PIECES

JAPANESE EGGPLANT TERIYAKI

∾ SMALL, slender Japanese eggplants, available in many well-stocked supermarkets and in Asian grocery stores, are best for this dish. Japanese sticky rice would be the traditional choice, but brown rice, or almost any variety, will complement the flavors of the teriyaki sauce.

4 small Japanese eggplant, stemmed and quartered lengthwise *— 1 regular*
1 garlic clove, minced
3 tablespoons fresh lemon juice
3 tablespoons tamari or other soy sauce
1 tablespoon honey (or other natural sweetener) *} good flavor*
2 tablespoons dark sesame oil
1 tablespoon vegetable oil
4 to 6 cups hot cooked Japanese sticky (glutinous) or *cut in half or dbl eggplant + sauce*
    short-grain brown rice

Place the eggplant quarters in a large shallow dish and pierce the skin of each in several places with a fork. In a small bowl, whisk together the garlic, lemon juice, tamari, and honey. Add the sesame oil in a slow, steady stream, whisking constantly until the mixture is emulsified and smooth. Pour the marinade over the eggplant, turning the eggplant to coat well. Allow the eggplant to marinate, turning occasionally, for at least 1 hour, or overnight in the refrigerator. When ready to cook, remove the eggplant from the marinade, reserving the marinade. Heat the vegetable oil in a large skillet over medium heat until hot. Add the eggplant and cook, turning once, until softened and browned on both sides, about 4 minutes. Add the reserved marinade and simmer, turning the eggplant once, for about 10 minutes, or until the eggplant is tender and the sauce is syrupy. Serve over the rice.

SERVES 4

Korean Rice with Daikon and Walnuts

♋ THIS flavorful topping, something like an Asian pesto, gets its refreshing crunch from daikon, a large white radish used in many Asian cuisines. Although long-grain white rice is suggested, try other varieties if you like.

2 cups long-grain white rice
3 ½ cups water
Salt
½ cup walnuts
1 cup peeled and sliced daikon
1 small hot green chile, halved lengthwise and seeded
1 teaspoon cider vinegar
Freshly ground black pepper to taste
1 teaspoon dark sesame oil
1 tablespoon finely chopped fresh parsley, for garnish

Preheat the oven to 350°F. In a medium saucepan, combine the rice, water, and ½ teaspoon salt and bring to a boil. Reduce the heat to low, cover, and simmer for 15 to 20 minutes, or until all the water is absorbed. While the rice is cooking, spread the walnuts on a baking sheet and bake, stirring once or twice, until lightly toasted, about 5 minutes. Let cool. In a food processor, pulse the daikon and chile until finely chopped. Add the walnuts and process to a coarse puree. Add in the vinegar and salt and pepper to taste and blend well; set aside. When the rice is cooked, remove from the heat, add the sesame oil, and fluff with a fork. Cover and let stand for 5 minutes. To serve, transfer the rice to a bowl and top with the walnut mixture and chopped parsley.

SERVES 4

RICETERA...
SHAPING RICE

THERE ARE A NUMBER of creative ways to serve rice for a special touch. For example, rice looks lovely on a platter when formed into a shape such as a round or oval. Use a lightly oiled ice cream scoop to shape the rice, or pack into a small ramekin, then unmold it. To make a display for a buffet table, choose larger molds in the appropriate shape and size.

CHAPTER 3

From Southeast Asia to India

Like their neighbors in China, Japan, and Korea, the people of Southeast Asia and India have an ancient relationship with rice and rely on it for their daily nourishment.

In Thailand, aromatic jasmine rice is favored. Some of the seasonings that define Thai food include lemongrass, cilantro, hot chiles, fish sauce, galangal (similar to ginger), and kaffir lime leaves. Thais also make use of aromatic Thai basil, holy basil, and cilantro, and they are noted for their hot and flavorful curries.

Vietnam and the countries of Indonesia also use lemongrass, cilantro, and fish sauce, but their cuisines, especially those of Indonesia, tend to be sweeter owing to their prolific use of coconut milk, nuts, and fruits, as in, for example, Coconut Cashew Rice.

On the Indian subcontinent, fragrant basmati rice provides a fluffy bed for lively curry dishes such as Indian Spiced Vegetables and other aromatic concoctions. Indian curries are distinctly different from Thai or other Asian curries, distinguished by the spices used in the curry mixture. Instead of the citrusy undertones of lemongrass and lime leaves, they have a deeper, more intense flavor from heady, fragrant spices such as cardamom, coriander seed, cumin, and turmeric.

THAI FRIED RICE

∽ FRESH bean sprouts and peanuts add a delightful crunch, and protein, to this quick and easy dish, made with fragrant jasmine rice and spicy basil. Thai basil can be found in Asian markets, but if it is unavailable, substitute regular basil. Fresh bean sprouts are also available in Asian markets and in well-stocked supermarkets. Thai birdseye chiles are super hot; you can substitute a milder variety, or even omit the chile if you prefer.

1 tablespoon vegetable oil
1 small onion, finely chopped
½ red bell pepper, finely chopped
½ cup grated carrots
1 garlic clove, minced
1 teaspoon minced fresh ginger
1 small Thai chile, minced (optional)
4 cups cold cooked jasmine rice
2 tablespoons tamari or other soy sauce
2 scallions, trimmed and finely minced
2 tablespoons minced fresh Thai basil
½ cup fresh bean sprouts
2 tablespoons chopped peanuts

Heat the oil in a large skillet or wok over medium-high heat until hot. Add the onion and stir-fry for 3 to 4 minutes, or until soft. Add the bell pepper, carrots, garlic, ginger, and chile, if using, and stir-fry for 2 minutes, or until slightly softened and fragrant. Add the rice and tamari and stir-fry for 3 minutes, or until the rice is heated through. Stir in the scallions and basil. Serve sprinkled with the bean sprouts and peanuts.

SERVES 4

Jasmine Rice with Slivered Tofu

ꙮ VEGETARIAN oyster sauce, also made from soy sauce, can be found in well-stocked Asian markets. If it's unavailable, just omit it—the dish will still be good.

1 pound extra-firm tofu, drained and blotted dry
2 tablespoons tamari or other soy sauce
1 tablespoon vegetarian oyster sauce
1 teaspoon light brown sugar
1 tablespoon vegetable oil
2 teaspoons minced garlic
½ to 2 Thai chiles (according to taste), thinly sliced
½ cup thinly sliced red onion
1 cup chopped fresh Thai basil
4 to 6 cups hot cooked jasmine rice

Cut the tofu into ¼-inch-thick slices and place on a baking sheet lined with paper towels to absorb excess liquid. Cover with more paper towels, place another baking sheet on top, and press down to extract excess water. Cut the tofu into matchstick slivers and set aside. Combine the tamari, oyster sauce, and sugar in a small bowl; set aside. Heat the oil in a large skillet or wok over medium-high heat until hot. Add the tofu, in batches if necessary, and cook, stirring until golden, about 30 seconds. Remove and set aside. Add the garlic and stir-fry for 10 seconds, or until fragrant. Add the chiles and onion and stir-fry for 30 seconds, or until softened. Add the tamari mixture, the basil, and the tofu and stir-fry for 1 minute, or until hot. Place the rice in a shallow serving bowl or on individual plates, top with the tofu mixture, and serve.

SERVES 4

VEGETABLES AND RICE WITH THAI PEANUT SAUCE

VARY the vegetables in this easy stir-fry according to personal preference and the season. To underscore the flavor of the peanut sauce, sprinkle on some chopped peanuts for garnish.

1 tablespoon vegetable oil
1 tablespoon minced garlic
1 small Thai chile, seeded and minced (optional)
½ cup chopped scallions
1 tablespoon finely chopped fresh ginger
2 tablespoons tamari or other soy sauce
½ cup water
1 teaspoon sugar
2 cups small cauliflower flowerets
1 pound green beans, trimmed and cut into 2-inch pieces
12 cherry tomatoes, halved
Thai Peanut Sauce (recipe follows)
5 to 6 cups hot cooked jasmine rice

Heat the oil in a large skillet or wok over medium-high heat until hot. Add the garlic, chile, if using, the scallions, and ginger and stir-fry for 1 minute, or until fragrant. Add the tamari, water, sugar, cauliflower, and green beans and stir and combine for 2 minutes, or until the vegetables begin to soften. Reduce the heat, cover, and simmer for 2 minutes longer, or until the vegetables are tender. Uncover, add the cherry tomatoes and Peanut Sauce, and toss gently to heat through. Serve at once over the hot cooked rice.

SERVES 4

Thai Peanut Sauce

BE FOREWARNED: This peanut sauce is addictive—you'll want to use it on everything. Try it as a dipping sauce for steamed fresh vegetables or spring rolls.

⅓ cup creamy peanut butter
¼ cup unsweetened coconut milk
1 tablespoon fresh lime juice
1 tablespoon tamari or other soy sauce
2 teaspoons light brown sugar
1 teaspoon Asian chile paste, or to taste

In a small bowl, whisk together the peanut butter, coconut milk, lime juice, tamari, brown sugar, and chile paste until well blended. Taste to adjust the seasoning. Use at once, or cover and refrigerate until ready to use. This sauce will keep well for up to a week. Bring to room temperature before using. For a thinner sauce, blend in a little water.

MAKES ABOUT ¾ CUP

THAI BASIL AND PEAS WITH JASMINE RICE

֍ THIS fragrantly flavorful dish takes only five minutes to cook—and only about that long to eat, if you use restraint! Look for Asian chile paste and Thai basil in Asian grocery stores.

2 teaspoons vegetable oil

2 tablespoons minced garlic

1 teaspoon Asian chile paste

2 tablespoons tamari or other soy sauce

1 tablespoon vegetarian "Fish Sauce" (recipe follows)

1 teaspoon light brown sugar

1 cup frozen peas, thawed

5 cups cold cooked jasmine rice

1 cup loosely packed fresh Thai basil leaves

1.5
2c raw

Heat the oil in large skillet or wok over medium-high heat until hot. Add the garlic and stir-fry for 30 seconds, or until fragrant. Add the chile paste, tamari, "fish sauce," and sugar and stir-fry for 30 seconds, or until well combined. Add the peas, rice, and basil and stir-fry for 3 to 4 minutes, or until heated through. Serve hot.

SERVES 4

Vegetarian "Fish Sauce"

KNOWN as *nam pla* in Thailand and *nuoc mam* in Vietnamese, fish sauce, made from salted and fermented fish, is a popular Thai seasoning. Traditional fish sauce is available in any Asian market, but this fish-free version is a reasonable substitute.

½ cup soy sauce
¼ cup water
1 tablespoon fresh lime juice
1 tablespoon sugar
½ teaspoon hot red pepper flakes

Combine the soy sauce, water, lime juice, sugar, and red pepper flakes in a small jar with a tight-fitting lid. Shake until well blended. Store in the refrigerator. It will keep for several weeks.

MAKES ABOUT ¾ CUP

COCONUT CASHEW RICE

∽ COCONUT is a frequent addition to rice dishes in areas of the world such as Indonesia where both crops are cultivated. Fragrant spices and the wonderful textures of the rich cashews and the coconut turn this easy dish into an elegant one. Unsweetened coconut is available in Asian markets and some natural food stores.

1 tablespoon vegetable oil
1 large onion, minced
2 garlic cloves, minced
4 scallions, trimmed and minced
1 tablespoon grated fresh ginger
½ teaspoon ground turmeric
½ teaspoon ground cinnamon
¼ teaspoon ground cloves
¼ teaspoon hot red pepper flakes
¼ cup unsweetened coconut milk
1 tablespoon sugar
5 cups cold cooked long-grain rice
½ cup shredded unsweetened coconut
Salt and freshly ground black pepper to taste
¼ cup chopped cashews, for garnish

Heat the oil in a large skillet or wok over medium heat until hot. Add the onion and garlic and cook until the onion is softened, about 5 minutes. Add the scallions, ginger, turmeric, cinnamon, cloves, red pepper flakes, coconut milk, and sugar and stir-fry over medium-high heat for 2 minutes, or until fragrant. Add the rice, stir to combine well, and heat until the rice is hot. Stir in the shredded coconut. Season to taste with salt and pepper. Transfer to a serving dish, sprinkle with the cashews, and serve.

SERVES 6

INDONESIAN RICE PATTIES

〜 THIS version of a popular Indonesian street food is delicious served with a traditional *sambal,* a hot and spicy relish. Many Asian markets offer a variety of sambals. The slightly sticky jasmine rice holds together well in patties; other good choices would be sticky rice or short-grain brown rice.

2½ cups cold cooked jasmine rice

1 cup finely chopped Napa cabbage

½ cup minced onion

½ cup shredded carrots

¼ cup chopped peanuts

1 garlic clove, minced

1 tablespoon soy sauce or kechap manis

1 tablespoon shredded unsweetened coconut

1 teaspoon light brown sugar

½ teaspoon ground cardamom

½ teaspoon ground cinnamon

Salt to taste

⅛ teaspoon cayenne, or to taste

Flour for dredging

1 tablespoon vegetable oil, or more if needed

Combine all the ingredients except the flour and oil in a food processor and process until well blended; transfer to a bowl. Scoop out about ½ cup of the mixture, shape it into a ¼-inch-thick patty, and place on a baking sheet. Repeat with the remaining mixture; you should have 6 to 8 patties. Lightly coat the patties with flour, shaking off the excess, and refrigerate for 5 minutes. Heat the oil in a large skillet over medium heat until hot. Add the patties, and cook, in batches if necessary, until lightly browned on both sides, about 3 minutes per side, adding additional oil if needed. Serve immediately.

SERVES 4

INDONESIAN FRIED RICE

∽ INDONESIAN fried rice, which has many versions, is called *Nasi Goreng*. It is traditionally made with *kechap* (also spelled *kecap*) *manis,* a sweet soy sauce found at Asian markets, and served with a spicy *sambal,* a traditional Indonesian condiment, also sold at Asian markets. If *kechap manis* is unavailable, substitute 2 tablespoons soy sauce combined with 2 teaspoons molasses.

2 cups broccoli flowerets
1 tablespoon vegetable oil
1 small onion, minced
4 cups cold cooked basmati or other long-grain white rice
Salt to taste
1 teaspoon Asian chile paste, or to taste
3 tablespoons kechap manis
1 tomato, diced
1 cucumber, peeled, halved lengthwise, seeded, and diced

Steam the broccoli over boiling water until just tender, about 3 to 5 minutes. Chop and set aside. Heat the oil in a large skillet or wok over medium heat until hot. Add the onion and cook until softened, about 3 minutes. Add the broccoli and rice, season with salt, and stir-fry until heated through, about 3 minutes. Add the chile paste, kechap manis, and tomato, toss to combine, and stir-fry until hot. Transfer to a serving bowl and top with the diced cucumber. Serve with a sambal and additional kechap manis on the side.

SERVES 4 TO 5

Vietnamese-Style Tempeh with Lemongrass and Cilantro

༄ VIETNAMESE cuisine is similar to Thai with its use of such ingredients as lemongrass and cilantro, but it tends to be sweeter and less spicy. Noodles, rice noodles that is, are extremely popular in Vietnam, but the Vietnamese also eat a great deal of jasmine and sticky rice.

One 2-inch piece lemongrass
1 tablespoon vegetable oil
8 ounces tempeh, cut into ½-inch cubes
½ cup thinly sliced red bell pepper
3 tablespoons Vegetarian "Fish Sauce" (page 39) or soy sauce
1 tablespoon rice vinegar
1 tablespoon light brown sugar
1 teaspoon Asian chile paste
4 scallions, trimmed and minced
4 to 6 cups hot cooked jasmine rice
3 tablespoons chopped fresh cilantro, for garnish

Remove the tough outer layer from the lemongrass and discard. Finely chop the remaining inner section and set aside. Heat the oil in a large skillet or wok over medium-high heat until hot. Add the tempeh and stir-fry until browned, about 4 minutes. Add the bell pepper and lemongrass and stir-fry for 1 minute. Add the "fish sauce," vinegar, sugar, chile paste, and scallions and stir to combine. Taste and adjust the seasoning if necessary. Spoon over the hot cooked rice and top with the chopped cilantro.

SERVES 4

INDIAN SPICED VEGETABLES
OVER BASMATI RICE

CHICKPEAS and rice, a favorite Indian combination, are featured in this spicy mélange, which also includes cabbage and carrots. Other vegetables, such as broccoli, cauliflower, or peas, may be added or substituted to suit personal taste.

1 tablespoon vegetable oil

1 large onion, thinly sliced

2 garlic cloves, minced

1 tablespoon minced fresh ginger

2 large carrots, cut on the diagonal into ¼-inch slices

3 cups shredded Napa cabbage

1½ cups cooked or canned chickpeas, rinsed if canned

¾ teaspoon ground cardamom

¼ teaspoon ground cinnamon

¼ teaspoon ground turmeric

½ teaspoon salt

⅛ teaspoon cayenne

½ cup water

1 cup unsweetened coconut milk

4 to 6 cups hot cooked basmati rice

Heat the oil in a large skillet or wok over medium heat until hot. Add the onion, garlic, and ginger and stir-fry until the onion is soft and lightly browned, about 7 minutes. Add the carrots, cabbage, chickpeas, cardamom, cinnamon, turmeric, salt, and pepper and stir-fry for 2 minutes, or until the vegetables are slightly softened. Add the water and bring to boil. Reduce the heat, cover, and simmer for about 15 minutes, or until the vegetables are tender. Stir in the coconut milk and heat through. Taste and adjust the seasonings if necessary. Serve over the hot cooked rice.

SERVES 4

CURRIED RICE AND VEGETABLES

❧ THIS Indian version of fried rice is a great way to stretch leftover rice into a delicious meal. Mango or another chutney makes a good—and traditional—accompaniment.

1 tablespoon vegetable oil
1 onion, finely chopped
2 teaspoon minced fresh ginger
1½ tablespoons Madras curry powder ← *cut in half w/ spicy curry + flavor is good!*
2 zucchini, cut into ½-inch dice (about 2 cups)
1 carrot, thinly sliced
¼ cup water, or more if needed
¾ cup frozen peas, thawed
3 cups cold cooked basmati rice
¼ cup chopped fresh parsley

Heat the oil in a large skillet or wok over medium heat until hot. Add the onion, cover, and cook, stirring occasionally, for 5 minutes, or until softened. Add the ginger and curry powder and stir-fry until fragrant, about 1 minute. Add the zucchini and carrot and stir-fry for about 1 minute, or until starting to soften. Lower the heat, add the water, cover, and cook for 2 minutes, or until the vegetables are tender; add an additional tablespoon or so of water if the pan becomes too dry. Uncover, add the peas, rice, and parsley, and cook uncovered, for 3 to 5 minutes, or until heated through. Serve immediately.

SERVES 4

VEGETABLE BIRYANI

BIRYANI, a classic dish of northern India, usually includes a variety of spices, lamb or other meat, vegetables, dried fruits, nuts, and basmati rice. It is traditionally baked as a layered casserole and makes a festive one-dish meal. Serve this vegetarian biryani with warmed naan bread and a spicy sweet chutney, available, along with the garam masala spice mixture, at Indian markets.

1 tablespoon vegetable oil
1 onion, diced
1 green bell pepper, diced
8 ounces green beans, trimmed and cut into 1-inch pieces
1 carrot, sliced thin
1 teaspoon minced fresh ginger
2 garlic cloves, minced
2 teaspoons garam masala (see headnote above), or to taste
½ teaspoon ground turmeric
½ teaspoon salt
¼ teaspoon cayenne
1½ cups basmati rice
4 cups water
1½ cups cooked or canned kidney beans, rinsed if canned
Peanuts, for garnish
Raisins, for garnish

Preheat the oven to 375°F. Heat the oil in a large ovenproof casserole over medium heat until hot. Add the onion, bell pepper, green beans, and carrot, and cook, stirring occasionally, until soft, about 10 minutes. Add the ginger, garlic, garam masala, turmeric, salt, and cayenne and cook for 2 minutes longer, stirring to combine. Stir in the rice, then stir in the water. Cover and bake for 30 minutes, or until the rice and vegetables are tender. Remove from the oven, stir in the kidney beans, replace the lid, and let stand for 5 minutes. Serve directly from the casserole, sprinkled with peanuts and raisins.

SERVES 4 TO 6

Rice and Lentils

A TRADITIONAL combination in India and the Middle East, lentils and rice make this wholesome, simple, but subtly spiced dish a powerhouse of protein. Serve with a salad or leafy green vegetable for a complete meal.

1 cup brown lentils, picked over and rinsed
1 tablespoon olive oil
1 large onion, minced
1 teaspoon ground cumin
1 teaspoon ground coriander
1 teaspoon minced fresh ginger
Salt and freshly ground black pepper to taste
1 ½ cups basmati rice

Bring a large saucepan of water to a boil, add the lentils, and cook for 10 minutes. Meanwhile, heat the oil in a large skillet over medium-high heat until hot. Add the onion and cook, stirring frequently, until lightly browned, about 7 to 10 minutes. Remove from the heat. Drain the lentils, return them to the saucepan, and add the cooked onion, cumin, coriander, ginger, and salt and pepper to taste. Add the rice and 4 cups water, bring to a boil, reduce the heat and simmer, covered, for about 20 minutes, until the lentils and rice are tender. Remove from the heat and allow to stand for 10 minutes before serving.

SERVES 4 TO 6

RICETERA...
SERVING RICE

TO MANY ASIAN PEOPLE, a bowl is the preferred vessel in which to serve rice, and chopsticks are the favored utensil. In China and other Asian countries, people often select toppings from a variety of bowls set family-style in the center of the table, flavoring their bowls of rice to their own individual tastes. They may then bring the bowl up to their mouth to eat at close range with chopsticks. In Thailand, chopsticks are traditionally used only for noodle dishes, and most people enjoy their rice-based meals served on small dinner plates, to be eaten with a spoon and fork. In some parts of India, and in other parts of Asia as well, people roll their rice into small balls and eat it with their hands. While Japan is famous for its sushi, or "rice sandwiches," the Japanese have special bowls for certain dishes, such as the donburi bowl, which is large enough to hold a generous serving of that delicious rice concoction (see page 26). In fact, *donburi* means "big bowl."

Other rice preparations are particularly suited to certain presentations. Italian risotto, for example, is usually served in shallow soup bowls or on plates. Pilafs are generally served on large platters, and paella is traditionally served from the special paella pan it cooks in. Indonesian festival rice is formed into a tall cylindrical shape and served on a platter.

CHAPTER 4

Global Innovation

Though we may associate it most strongly with Asia, rice is also a common denominator of many of the world's other cuisines. The countries of the Middle East, for example, employ this ancient grain most notably in their stuffed vegetable dishes and fruity pilafs, such as Persian Rice Pilaf. It was in African nations such as Senegal and Nigeria that many of our American and Caribbean rice traditions originated, later brought to the West by African slaves. Nigerian Black-Eyed Peas might be considered a precursor to the all-American Hoppin' John. Then there are the uniquely European ways with rice, such as the creamy risottos of Italy, Greek spanakorizo, and zesty Spanish paella.

Rice with Lemon-Tahini Sauce

Tahini, or sesame paste, combined with chickpeas, garlic, and lemon juice makes a hummus-like sauce that is glorious over any type of rice, particularly fragrant basmati or another long-grain variety.

1 ½ cups cooked or canned chickpeas, rinsed if canned
1 large garlic clove, coarsely chopped
½ cup tahini
¼ cup fresh lemon juice
3 tablespoons tamari or other soy sauce
⅛ teaspoon cayenne
¼ to ½ cup water
4 to 6 cups hot cooked basmati or Texmati, or other long-grain rice
2 tablespoons chopped fresh parsley, for garnish
1 tablespoon toasted sesame seeds, for garnish

In a food processor, combine the chickpeas and garlic and pulse until finely minced. Add the tahini, lemon juice, tamari, and cayenne and process until smooth. Transfer the mixture to a saucepan and heat slowly over low heat, whisking in just enough water to reach the desired consistency. Taste and adjust the seasoning if necessary. Spoon the sauce over the hot cooked rice, garnish with the parsley and toasted sesame seeds, and serve immediately.

SERVES 4

Persian Rice Pilaf

   Nutty basmati rice is a good complement to the sweetness of the raisins and cinnamon in this Middle Eastern pilaf.

2 tablespoons olive oil
1 onion, minced
1½ cups basmati or other long-grain rice
⅓ cup golden raisins or chopped dried apricots
1 teaspoon paprika
3 cups hot vegetable stock or water
½ teaspoon ground cinnamon
Salt to taste
⅛ teaspoon cayenne
3 tablespoons toasted slivered almonds
2 tablespoons minced fresh parsley

Heat the oil in a large skillet over low heat until hot. Add the onion, cover, and cook for about 7 minutes, or until soft. Increase the heat to medium, add the rice, raisins or apricots, and paprika and cook for 2 minutes, stirring to coat the rice with the oil. Pour the hot stock or water over the rice mixture, season with the cinnamon, salt, and cayenne, stir to combine, and cover. Reduce the heat to low, and simmer gently for 20 minutes, or until the rice is tender and all the water is absorbed. Remove from the heat and allow to stand for 5 minutes. Fluff the rice with a fork, stir in the almonds and the parsley, and serve.

SERVES 4

FAVA BEANS AND RICE WITH LEMON-MINT PESTO SAUCE

ᏊᎧ FRESH mint, lemon juice, and almonds make a fragrant Middle Eastern version of pesto that provides a lively counterpoint to the delicate rice and meaty fava beans. Almost any type of rice would work beautifully in this dish. Try to find delicious fresh young fava beans, but if they are unavailable, dried or canned favas can be substituted.

2 large garlic cloves
½ teaspoon salt
½ cup whole unblanched almonds
1 cup fresh mint leaves
½ cup fresh parsley leaves
3 tablespoons fresh lemon juice
¾ cup olive oil
5 to 6 cups Wehani, basmati, or other hot cooked rice
1½ cups cooked (see Note) or canned fava beans, rinsed if canned

used can of
large size beans
?azurka?

Combine the garlic, salt, and almonds in a food processor and pulse until blended to a paste. Add the mint and parsley and pulse, scraping down the sides of the bowl as needed. Add the lemon juice and pulse to blend. With the machine running, slowly add the olive oil, processing until emulsified and smooth. To serve, toss the sauce with the hot cooked rice and fava beans.

NOTE: If you can find fresh fava beans, you will need about 3 pounds favas in the pod to yield 1½ cups beans. Fresh favas have tough skins and should be blanched for 1 minute to remove them before cooking. You can then easily pop them out of their skins with your finger. Once the skins are removed, favas can then be cooked in lightly salted water for 5 to 10 minutes, depending on the size of the beans. If using dried beans, soak them overnight in water to cover, then drain and cook in a large pot of boiling water for about 1½ hours, or until tender; do not add salt to the cooking water until the beans are almost done, or they will toughen.

SERVES 4

GREEK RICE AND SPINACH

GⓄ *SPANAKORIZO*, or "spinach rice," can be made with either long- or short-grain rice, depending on your preference for the texture of the dish, but I prefer the appearance of the fluffy separate grains of long-grain varieties here. Try it garnished with chopped ripe tomatoes or crumbled feta, or both.

1 tablespoon olive oil
1 small onion, finely chopped
2 bunches spinach (about 1 pound), trimmed and washed,
    coarsely chopped
1 ½ cups long- or short-grain white rice
3 cups vegetable stock or water
1 teaspoon minced fresh oregano or ¼ teaspoon dried
½ teaspoon salt
⅛ teaspoon freshly ground black pepper
Pinch of ground nutmeg
3 tablespoons chopped fresh mint

Heat the oil in a large skillet over medium heat until hot. Add the onion and cook for 5 minutes, or until softened. Add the spinach and cook until wilted, about 2 minutes. Add the rice, stock or water, oregano, salt, pepper, and nutmeg, and bring to a boil. Reduce the heat to low, cover, and simmer for 15 to 20 minutes, or until the rice is tender and all the liquid has been absorbed. Stir in the mint, remove from the heat, and allow to stand for 5 minutes. Fluff with a fork and serve.

SERVES 4

VEGETABLE TAGINE

∽∾ THIS flavorful Moroccan stew is named for the earthenware pot in which it is cooked. It is traditionally made with meat, preserved lemons or other fruit, and heady spices. Here, chickpeas stand in for the meat. Tagines are usually served with couscous, but rice—almost any variety of rice could be enjoyed with this dish—makes a nice change of pace.

1 tablespoon olive oil
1 large onion, chopped
1 carrot, chopped
1 zucchini, diced
1 garlic clove, minced
½ teaspoon ground cinnamon
½ teaspoon ground turmeric
¼ teaspoon cayenne
1 (16-ounce) can diced tomatoes
2 cups vegetable stock or water
Salt, to taste
½ cup dried apricots
¼ cup raisins
Zest of 1 lemon
2½ cups cooked or canned chickpeas, rinsed if canned
2 tablespoons minced fresh cilantro or parsley
6 cups hot cooked brown basmati or other rice

Heat the oil in a large saucepan over medium heat until hot. Add the onion and carrot and cook, covered, for 5 minutes, or until softened. Add the zucchini, garlic, cinnamon, turmeric, salt, cayenne, tomatoes, stock or water, and salt to taste. Reduce the heat to low, and simmer for 25 minutes. Meanwhile, soak the apricots in hot water for 20 minutes, then drain and finely chop. Add the apricots, raisins, lemon zest, and chickpeas to the vegetable mixture and cook 5 minutes longer, or until hot and the flavors are blended. Stir in the cilantro or parsley and serve over the rice.

SERVES 4 TO 6

NIGERIAN BLACK-EYED PEAS

THIS recipe was inspired by a Nigerian dish called *wake-ewa*, which is made with black-eyed peas. I like to serve it over short-grain brown rice to complement the robust flavors of the dish, but any rice can be used.

1 tablespoon olive oil

1 large onion, chopped

1 teaspoon chili powder

1 teaspoon dried thyme

1 teaspoon ground coriander

1 (16-ounce) can diced tomatoes

½ teaspoon sugar

Salt to taste

1½ to 2 cups cooked or canned black-eyed peas,
  rinsed if canned

4 to 6 cups short-grain brown, brown basmati,
  or other hot cooked rice

Heat the oil in a large skillet over medium heat until hot. Add the onion and cook for 5 minutes, or until softened. Stir in the chili powder, thyme, coriander, tomatoes, sugar, and salt to taste. Reduce the heat to low and simmer for 5 minutes, stirring frequently; add a little water if the mixture becomes too dry. Add the beans and cook 5 minutes longer to heat through and blend the flavors. Serve over the hot rice.

SERVES 4

Risotto Primavera

🌀 RED PEPPER, carrots, and zucchini add color, texture, and flavor to this creamy risotto. Serve it in shallow soup bowls, with a crisp salad and warm garlic bread for a satisfying meal. While arborio rice is the most readily available in the United States, carnaroli and vialone nano are also highly prized risotto rices.

4½ cups vegetable stock or water
1 tablespoon olive oil
½ cup finely chopped red bell pepper
½ cup grated carrots
1 cup shredded zucchini
2 garlic cloves, minced
1½ cups arborio rice
¼ cup dry white wine
Salt and freshly ground black pepper to taste
¼ cup chopped fresh parsley
1 tablespoon fresh lemon juice

In a medium saucepan, bring the stock or water to a simmer; reduce the heat to low and keep at a simmer. Heat the olive oil in a large saucepan over medium heat until hot. Add the bell pepper, carrots, zucchini, and garlic and sauté for 5 minutes. Add the rice, and stir to coat with oil. Add the wine and simmer gently, stirring occasionally, until it has been absorbed. Add ½ cup of the stock or water and cook, stirring constantly, until all the liquid has been absorbed. Adjust the heat as necessary to maintain a simmer. Continue cooking, adding stock or water ½ cup at a time and stirring until it is absorbed, until the rice is tender but still firm and the risotto is thick and creamy, about 25 minutes (you may not need all the stock or water). Add salt and pepper to taste, then add the parsley and lemon juice. Adjust the seasoning if necessary. Serve immediately.

SERVES 4 TO 6

RISOTTO WITH ARTICHOKES AND MUSHROOMS

ITALIAN porcini mushrooms, also called cèpes, add a rich flavor and an authentic touch to this elegant risotto. Although expensive, the results are well worth it. These mushrooms are available seasonally at specialty markets and many well-stocked supermarkets. If unavailable, substitute creminis, portobellos, or white button mushrooms.

4 cups vegetable stock or water
¼ cup dry white wine
2 tablespoons olive oil
1 small onion, minced
1½ cups arborio rice
1 cup chopped porcini or other mushrooms (see headnote above)
1 cup drained marinated artichoke hearts, chopped
½ teaspoon salt
Freshly ground black pepper to taste

Combine the stock or water and wine in a medium saucepan and bring to a simmer; reduce the heat to low and keep at a simmer.

In a large saucepan, heat the oil over medium heat until hot. Add the onion and sauté, stirring frequently, until soft and golden brown, about 5 minutes. Add the rice and mushrooms and stir until coated with oil and the rice turns translucent. Sauté for 5 minutes. Add the rice, stir to coat with oil.

Add the wine and simmer gently, stirring occasionally, until it has been absorbed. Add ½ cup of the stock or water and cook, stirring constantly, until all the liquid has been absorbed. Adjust the heat as necessary to maintain a simmer. Continue cooking, adding stock or water ½ cup at a time and stirring until it is absorbed, until the rice is tender but still firm and the risotto is thick and creamy, about 25 minutes (you may not need all the stock or water).

About 10 minutes before the rice is finished, stir in the marinated artichoke hearts. When the risotto is finished, remove from the heat and season with the salt and pepper to taste. Serve immediately in shallow bowls.

SERVES 4

PESTO RISOTTO

∽ Two of Italy's most sublime creations pair up in this feast for the senses. I like to serve this risotto with grilled portobello mushrooms, accompanied by a crisp Sauvignon Blanc.

4 cups vegetable stock or water
2 tablespoons olive oil
½ cup minced onion
1½ cups arborio rice
¼ cup dry white wine
3 tablespoons Basil Pesto (recipe follows)
½ teaspoon salt
Freshly ground black pepper to taste

In a medium saucepan, bring the stock or water to a simmer; keep at a simmer over low heat. In a large saucepan, heat the oil over medium heat until hot. Add the onion and cook for 5 minutes, or until soft. Add the rice and stir for 1 minute, or until well coated with oil and slightly translucent. Add ½ cup of the simmering stock and cook, stirring constantly, until the rice has absorbed most of the liquid. Add the wine and simmer gently, stirring occasionally, until it has been absorbed. Add ½ cup of the stock or water and cook, stirring constantly, until all the liquid has been absorbed. Adjust the heat as necessary to maintain a simmer. Continue cooking, adding stock or water ½ cup at a time and stirring until it is absorbed, until the rice is tender but still firm and the risotto is thick and creamy, about 25 minutes (you may not need all the stock or water). Add the pesto and season with the salt and pepper. Serve immediately.

SERVES 4

Basil Pesto

P E S T O is one of the best reasons I know to grow lots of fresh basil. Because it is made without cheese, this pesto can be stashed in the freezer for future use. To freeze, place it in a small container, top with a thin layer of olive oil, and cover with a tight-fitting lid.

3 cups fresh basil leaves
2 to 3 garlic cloves
⅓ cup pine nuts
¾ teaspoon salt
⅓ cup olive oil

Place the basil leaves in a food processor with the garlic and process until finely minced. Add the pine nuts and salt and process to a puree. With the processor running, slowly add the oil, processing to a paste. Taste and adjust the seasoning if necessary.

M A K E S   A B O U T   1 ½   C U P S

Bell Peppers Stuffed with Rice, Spinach, and Sun-Dried Tomatoes

∂∿ The rich flavor of these stuffed peppers is enhanced by the smoky sweetness of the sun-dried tomatoes. The rice mixture can also be used to stuff zucchini or other vegetables or enjoyed on its own.

4 large bell peppers (red, yellow, or green)
½ cup sun-dried tomatoes packed in olive oil
1 tablespoon olive oil
1 large bunch spinach, washed, trimmed, and coarsely chopped
1 garlic clove, minced
3 to 4 cups cooked long-grain white or brown rice
1 tablespoon minced fresh parsley
¼ teaspoon salt
⅛ teaspoon freshly ground black pepper

Preheat the oven to 350°F. Slice off the tops of the peppers and remove the seeds and membranes. Plunge the peppers into a pot of boiling water and cook for 2 to 3 minutes, or until slightly softened. Remove the peppers from the water and set aside, cut side down, to drain. Chop the tomatoes and set aside. Heat the oil in a large skillet over medium heat until hot. Add the spinach, garlic, and tomatoes and cook until the spinach is wilted, 2 to 3 minutes. Add the rice, parsley, salt, and pepper and stir to combine. Fill the peppers with the rice mixture and place upright in a baking dish. Add a few tablespoons of water to the baking dish, cover, and bake until the filling is hot and the peppers are tender, about 20 minutes. Serve hot.

SERVES 4

Rice with Puttanesca Sauce

෴ This fresh, uncooked version of a classic pasta sauce is also delicious served over rice. The rich nutty flavor of brown rice stands up well to the piquant flavors of the sauce. If you prefer a cooked sauce, you can sauté the garlic and tomatoes in the olive oil, then add the remaining ingredients except the rice and heat through.

2 pounds ripe plum tomatoes, chopped (about 4 cups)
½ cup black Kalamata olives, pitted and sliced
½ cup green olives, pitted and sliced
2 tablespoons capers, rinsed and drained
1 tablespoon minced garlic
2 tablespoons olive oil
¼ cup chopped fresh basil
1 tablespoon minced fresh parsley
½ teaspoon salt
¼ teaspoon hot red pepper flakes
4 to 6 cups hot cooked short- or long-grain brown or other rice

In a large bowl, combine the tomatoes, olives, capers, garlic, and oil. Add the basil, parsley, salt, and red pepper flakes, stirring to combine. Cover and let stand at room temperature for 20 to 30 minutes, stirring occasionally. Serve over the hot cooked rice.

SERVES 4

PORTOBELLOS OVER RICE

❧❧ M O S T any rice variety will complement this flavorful mushroom sauté with sweet red peppers, but you might want to try a packaged rice blend, or perhaps a combination of long-grain white rice and wild rice.

1 tablespoon olive oil
1 garlic clove, minced
4 large portobello mushroom caps, sliced
½ red bell pepper, cut into strips
1 tablespoon capers, rinsed and drained
2 tablespoons dry white wine
1 tablespoon fresh lemon juice
1 tablespoon chopped fresh parsley
1 teaspoon minced fresh marjoram or ¼ teaspoon dried
Salt and freshly ground black pepper to taste
4 to 6 cups hot cooked rice (see headnote above)

Heat the oil in a large skillet over medium heat until hot. Add the garlic, portobello slices, and bell pepper strips and sauté for 2 minutes. Add the capers, wine, lemon juice, parsley, marjoram, and salt and pepper and cook 2 minutes longer. Serve over the hot cooked rice.

S E R V E S 4

Risi Bisi

Easier than a risotto, this classic rice and pea combination, made with arborio rice, is a favorite Italian comfort food. For added flavor, top with finely chopped lightly browned vegetarian Canadian bacon, available at natural food stores and many supermarkets.

1 tablespoon olive oil
½ cup minced onion
1¼ cups arborio rice
3¾ cups vegetable stock or water
½ teaspoon salt
⅛ teaspoon freshly ground black pepper
1½ cups fresh or frozen green peas
1 tablespoon chopped fresh parsley, for garnish

Heat the olive oil in large skillet over medium heat until hot. Add the onion and cook until softened, about 5 minutes. Reduce the heat to low. Stir in the rice, the stock or water, and salt and pepper, bring to a simmer, and simmer for 20 minutes, stirring frequently. Add the peas and cook, stirring frequently, for 5 minutes longer, or until the rice is soft. Adjust the seasoning if necessary, sprinkle with the chopped parsley, and serve.

SERVES 4

Vegetable Paella

While paella generally includes meat and/or seafood, this vegetarian rendition brims with vegetables and derives its protein from meaty cannellini beans. Paella is traditionally made with Spanish Valencia rice, which can be found in specialty food shops. If unavailable, arborio rice may be substituted. In any case, use a short-grain rice for authenticity. The saffron is traditional, but turmeric can be used to create the same golden color at a fraction of the cost.

2 tablespoons olive oil
1 medium onion, chopped
1 red bell pepper, diced
8 ounces green beans, trimmed and cut into 1-inch pieces
1 (28-ounce) can plum tomatoes, drained and chopped
2 garlic cloves, finely chopped
4 cups vegetable stock or water
1½ cups Valencia or other short-grain rice
¼ teaspoon ground fennel
Pinch of saffron threads or ¼ teaspoon ground turmeric
½ teaspoon salt
½ teaspoon hot red pepper flakes
1½ to 2 cups cooked or canned cannellini beans, rinsed if canned
1 cup frozen peas, thawed

Preheat the oven to 375°F. Heat the oil in a large ovenproof skillet or saucepan over medium heat until hot. Add the onion, bell pepper, and green beans and cook for 5 minutes, or until softened. Stir in the tomatoes, garlic, and stock or water and bring to a boil, then stir in the rice, fennel, saffron or turmeric, salt, and hot pepper flakes. Remove from the heat, cover, and place in the oven. Bake for 30 minutes, or until the rice is tender. Remove from the oven, stir in the cannellini beans and peas, cover, and let stand for 10 minutes before serving.

SERVES 4 TO 6

Arroz con Tempeh

 The firm, meaty texture of tempeh makes it well suited as the substitute for chicken in this vegetarian version of the Spanish classic Arroz con Pollo.

1 tablespoon olive oil
8 ounces tempeh, cut into 1-inch pieces
1 onion, chopped
1 red bell pepper, chopped
1 small carrot, chopped
2 garlic cloves, chopped
½ teaspoon dried oregano
½ teaspoon ground cumin
⅛ teaspoon saffron threads or ground turmeric
1¼ cups Valencia or other short-grain rice
1 (16-ounce) can diced tomatoes
3½ cups vegetable stock or water
8 ounces green beans, trimmed and cut into 1-inch lengths
Salt to taste
½ cup frozen peas, thawed
⅓ cup pimiento-stuffed green olives
¼ cup prepared salsa
Freshly ground black pepper to taste

Heat the oil in a large saucepan over medium heat until hot. Add the tempeh, onion, bell pepper, and carrot, cover, and cook for 5 minutes, or until the vegetables are softened. Add the garlic, oregano, cumin, and saffron or turmeric and sauté for 1 to 2 minutes longer. Stir in the rice, add the tomatoes, stock or water, green beans, and salt to taste, cover, and simmer for 20 to 25 minutes, or until the rice is tender. Add the peas, olives, and salsa, season with pepper to taste, and cook for about 5 minutes, until heated through. Taste and adjust the seasonings before serving.

SERVES 4

Provençal Vegetables and Rice

⚬ Ratatouille, the classic vegetable stew from Provence, makes a perfect topping for rice. And since ratatouille, like many stews, tastes even better the day after it's made, make both it and your rice ahead, for a convenient meal that's ready to heat up in a flash. Any rice tastes great topped with this flavorful mélange, so feel free to experiment.

1 tablespoon olive oil

1 small eggplant, cut into ½-inch cubes

1 onion, diced

1 red bell pepper, cut into ½-inch pieces

2 garlic cloves, minced

2 small zucchini, cut into ½-inch cubes

2 cups chopped tomatoes (fresh or canned)

2 tablespoons chopped fresh parsley

1 tablespoon chopped fresh basil

1 teaspoon minced fresh thyme

1 teaspoon salt

⅛ teaspoon cayenne

6 cups hot cooked rice

Heat the oil in a large saucepan over medium heat until hot. Add the eggplant and onion, cover, and cook for 5 minutes, or until softened. Add the bell pepper and garlic, cover, and cook, stirring occasionally, for 5 minutes longer or until soft. Add the zucchini, tomatoes, parsley, basil, thyme, salt, and cayenne and cook for 15 minutes, or until all the vegetables are tender. Taste and adjust the seasoning. Serve over the hot cooked rice.

SERVES 4

RICE-STUFFED CABBAGE ROLLS

∞ THESE flavorful cabbage bundles are a classic in Eastern European cooking. When I was a child, my mother made them for me stuffed with barley, but rice is also frequently used. I especially like the way short-grain brown rice holds together in the savory packets. For a different flavor, a cup of tomato sauce may be used instead of the apple juice, but the apple juice will add a subtle sweetness to the dish.

1 head cabbage, cored

2 tablespoons olive oil

1 onion, chopped

½ cup raisins, soaked in warm water for 10 minutes
    and drained

2 tablespoons minced fresh parsley

¼ teaspoon ground allspice

⅛ teaspoon ground cinnamon

½ teaspoon salt

¼ teaspoon freshly ground black pepper

⅛ teaspoon cayenne

1 tablespoon fresh lemon juice

3 cups cooked short-grain brown rice

1 cup water

½ cup apple juice

Place the cabbage in a large pot with a steamer rack and enough salted water to come just to the bottom of the rack. Cover and steam until the first few outer layers of leaves are softened, about 10 minutes. Remove as many of the cabbage leaves that are soft and lay them out rib side down on a work surface. Return the cabbage to the steamer for 5 minutes to soften more leaves for a total of 12 leaves. Meanwhile, heat 1 tablespoon of the olive oil in a large skillet over medium heat until hot. Add the onion and cook, covered, for 5 minutes, or until softened. Add the raisins, parsley, allspice, cinnamon, salt, black pepper, and cayenne, stirring to combine. Transfer to a bowl, add the lemon juice and rice, and mix well.

Preheat the oven to 350°F. Lightly oil a 9 × 13-inch baking pan.

Place approximately ⅓ cup of the stuffing mixture on each cabbage leaf on the work surface. Fold the bottom of each leaf up over the stuffing, then fold over the sides and roll up into a neat packet. Place the filled cabbage rolls seam side down in the baking pan. Drizzle with the remaining 1 tablespoon olive oil, and add the water and apple juice. Bake, covered, for 45 minutes, or until the stuffing is heated through and the leaves are very tender. Serve with the liquid from the pan.

SERVES 4 TO 6

CUBAN BLACK BEANS AND RICE

⌒◯ THE Spanish name for this classic Cuban dish is *moros y cristianos,* or "Moors and Christians." My version is ready in minutes with the help of canned black beans and already cooked rice. For authenticity, use a long-grain white rice.

1 tablespoon vegetable oil
1 onion, finely chopped
½ green bell pepper, minced
2 garlic cloves, minced
1 jalapeño chile, seeded and minced (optional)
½ teaspoon ground cumin
¼ teaspoon dried oregano
1 (16-ounce) can diced tomatoes, drained
1½ cups cooked or canned black beans, rinsed if canned
½ teaspoon salt
Freshly ground black pepper to taste
4 to 6 cups hot cooked long-grain white rice

Heat the oil in a large saucepan over medium heat until hot. Add the onion, bell pepper, garlic, and jalapeño, if using, cover, and cook for 5 minutes, or until the vegetables begin to soften. Stir in the cumin and oregano and cook for 1 minute, or until fragrant. Add the tomatoes, beans, salt, and pepper, cover, and simmer, stirring occasionally, for 15 minutes, or until the vegetables are tender. Taste and adjust the seasoning, spoon over the hot rice, and serve.

SERVES 4 TO 6

Tempeh Picadillo

TEMPEH replaces ground beef in this Mexican favorite, which combines sweet apples and raisins with olives, garlic, and hot chiles for a symphony of flavors and textures. Various brands of crumbled vegetarian burgers are available in supermarkets and natural food stores and can be substituted for the tempeh. Long-grain white rice is traditional.

1 tablespoon olive oil
1 onion, chopped
1 small green bell pepper, minced
8 ounces tempeh, grated
2 garlic cloves, chopped
1 jalapeño chile, chopped
1 (16-ounce) can diced tomatoes
1 Granny Smith apple, peeled and chopped
½ cup raisins
¼ cup sliced pitted black olives
Salt and freshly ground black pepper to taste
3½ cups hot cooked long-grain white, Texmati, or other rice
2 tablespoons chopped fresh parsley, for garnish
2 tablespoons toasted slivered almonds, for garnish

Heat the oil in a large skillet over medium heat until hot. Add the onion, bell pepper, tempeh, garlic, and chile and cook, stirring occasionally, for 5 minutes, or until the vegetables are soft and the tempeh is golden brown. Stir in the tomatoes, apple, raisins, olives, and salt and pepper to taste. Simmer for 15 minutes, stirring occasionally, until the flavors are well blended. Add a little water if the mixture becomes too dry. To serve, stir the rice into the tempeh mixture, transfer to a large shallow serving bowl, and garnish with the chopped parsley and slivered almonds.

SERVES 4

Jamaican-Style Rice and Peas

ALTHOUGH there are many variations of this traditional dish throughout the Caribbean, it's a special favorite in Jamaica, where the "peas" used are actually red kidney beans. Coconut milk and chile peppers add richness and heat to this tasty and nutritious version, which can be ready in minutes if using cooked rice and canned beans. Serve with a salad or green vegetable for a complete meal.

1 tablespoon olive oil
1 onion, chopped
2 garlic cloves, chopped
1 to 2 small hot chiles, seeded and chopped
1 teaspoon minced fresh thyme or ½ teaspoon dried
1 cup unsweetened coconut milk
4 cups cooked long-grain white rice
1½ cups cooked or canned red kidney beans, rinsed if canned
Salt and freshly ground black pepper to taste

Heat the oil in a large skillet over medium heat until hot. Add the onion, garlic, and chiles and cook for 5 minutes, or until the vegetables soften. Add the thyme and coconut milk, stirring to combine, then stir in the rice and beans and season with salt and pepper to taste. Cook over low heat, stirring gently, until heated through, about 5 minutes. Serve in a shallow bowl.

SERVES 4

Caribbean Pilau with Jerk-Spiced Vegetables

୬୬ FRESH vegetables and zesty spices are the keynote of this flavorful Island dish. I like it with brown or white basmati rice, but any long-grain rice will do nicely.

2 tablespoons olive oil

1 small onion, finely chopped

2 garlic cloves, minced

1 small red chile, seeded and minced

1 teaspoon minced fresh ginger

1 cup brown or white basmati or other long-grain rice

½ teaspoon ground allspice

¼ teaspoon dried thyme

¼ teaspoon ground nutmeg

⅛ teaspoon ground turmeric

¾ teaspoon salt

¼ teaspoon freshly ground black pepper

2 cups hot vegetable stock or water

½ teaspoon light brown sugar (or a natural sweetener to taste)

⅛ teaspoon cayenne

1 red bell pepper, cut into ½-inch dice

2 zucchini, cut into ½-inch slices

8 ounces white mushrooms, trimmed and quartered

Heat 1 tablespoon of the oil in a large saucepan over medium heat until hot. Add the onion, garlic, chile, and ginger and cook until the onion is softened, about 5 minutes. Add the rice, stirring to coat with oil, then add ¼ teaspoon of the allspice, ⅛ teaspoon each of the thyme and nutmeg, the turmeric, ½ teaspoon of the salt, and ⅛ teaspoon of the pepper, mixing to combine. Add the hot stock or water, cover, and cook until the rice is tender and the liquid is absorbed, about 15 to 20 minutes. While the rice is cooking, in a small bowl, combine the remaining ¼ teaspoon allspice, ⅛ teaspoon each nutmeg and thyme, ¼ teaspoon salt, ⅛ teaspoon pepper, and the sugar and cayenne; set aside. Heat the remaining 1 tablespoon oil in a large skillet over medium heat. Add the bell pepper, zucchini, and mushrooms and cook, stirring occasionally, for 5 minutes, or until beginning to soften. Sprinkle the reserved spice mixture over the vegetables, toss until evenly coated, and continue cooking until the vegetables are tender, about 5 minutes. Serve the vegetables over the rice pilau.

SERVES 4

RICETERA...
WHAT GIVES AROMATIC RICES THEIR AROMA?

YOU WOULD THINK that the captivating flavor and scent of aromatic rices such as basmati and jasmine would have a romantic or exotic name. Not so. The component responsible for the sensory delight is 2-acetyl pyroline; in aromatic rices there's ten times more of this compound than in other rice varieties.

CHAPTER 5

American Fusion

What Americans lack in ancient traditions, we make up for in ingenuity, as we borrow from global cultures to enjoy rice in its many guises. Not that we don't have some terrific rice dishes of our own, although most of what are considered classic American recipes were actually brought over from Africa in the 1700s. Since rice is grown predominantly in the South, we look to Louisiana and other Southern states for our traditional rice dishes, such as Jambalaya, Louisiana Red Beans and Rice, Hoppin' John, and Red Beans and Rice. In addition to meatless versions of these familiar favorites, this chapter contains a number of unique new dishes like Rice and Vegetable Hash, Succotash Sauté, and Southern Fried Rice.

Louisiana Red Beans and Rice

〰️ Also known as "Monday night supper" in New Orleans, where virtually every kitchen has a spicy pot of kidney beans simmering on the stove come Monday. Filé powder is made from ground sassafras leaves and is used to season and thicken gumbos and other Creole dishes. It is available in specialty food shops and in the gourmet section of well-stocked supermarkets.

1 tablespoon vegetable oil

1 onion, finely chopped

1 small green bell pepper, finely chopped

2 garlic cloves, minced

1 (28-ounce) can diced tomatoes, drained

3 cups cooked or canned kidney beans, rinsed if canned

½ cup water

1 teaspoon filé powder

1 teaspoon Tabasco sauce

1 teaspoon dried thyme, crumbled

½ teaspoon salt

⅛ teaspoon cayenne

1 bay leaf

4 to 6 cups hot cooked long-grain white rice (or try Louisiana pecan rice)

Heat the oil in a large saucepan over medium heat until hot. Add the onion, bell pepper, and garlic and sauté until tender, about 10 minutes. Add the tomatoes, kidney beans, water, filé powder, Tabasco sauce, thyme, salt, and cayenne. Cover and simmer until the flavors have blended, about 10 minutes. Serve over the rice.

SERVES 4

Jambalaya

Jambalaya is traditionally made with meat or seafood and served over long-grain white rice. Since this meatless version breaks with tradition in any case, try it with brown rice instead. Tempeh and vegetarian sausage links are available in natural food stores and well-stocked supermarkets.

1 tablespoon vegetable oil
1 small onion, coarsely chopped
½ cup coarsely chopped celery
1 green bell pepper, coarsely chopped
1 garlic clove, minced
2 (16-ounce) cans diced tomatoes
2 tablespoons tomato paste
1 teaspoon filé powder
1 tablespoon chopped fresh parsley
1 teaspoon Tabasco sauce
1 teaspoon salt
½ cup water
1½ cups cooked or canned pinto beans, rinsed if canned
4 ounces tempeh, cubed
8 ounces vegetarian sausage links, cut into 1-inch pieces
6 cups long-grain brown, or Wehani, or other hot cooked rice

In a large pot, heat 1½ teaspoons of the oil over medium heat until hot. Add the onion, celery, and bell pepper and sauté for 5 minutes, or until the vegetables begin to soften. Add the garlic, tomatoes, tomato paste, filé powder, parsley, Tabasco sauce, salt, and water. Cover and simmer for 20 minutes, or until the vegetables are soft. Stir in the pinto beans. Meanwhile, heat the remaining 1½ teaspoons oil in a large skillet over medium-high heat. Add the tempeh and vegetarian sausage and cook until browned, about 5 minutes. Add the tempeh and sausage to the tomato mixture and simmer for about 5 minutes, until the flavors are well blended. Adjust the seasonings. Serve over the hot cooked rice.

SERVES 4 TO 6

GREENS AND BEANS RAGOUT

CANNELLINI beans and iron-rich greens make a tasty and nutritious topping for rice. You could substitute spinach, escarole, chard, or collards for the kale, or use a combination. Long-grain white or brown rice is a good choice for this dish.

1 tablespoon olive oil

1 onion, finely chopped

2 garlic cloves, finely minced

4 cups coarsely chopped kale (or other dark leafy greens;
    see headnote above)

½ teaspoon salt

⅛ teaspoon cayenne

1 tablespoon white wine vinegar

1 cup water

2½ cups cooked or canned cannellini beans, rinsed if canned

4 to 6 cups hot cooked long-grain brown or white rice

Heat the oil in a large pot over medium heat until hot. Add the onion and garlic and cook for 5 minutes, or until soft. Add the kale, salt, cayenne, vinegar, and water and bring to a boil. Reduce the heat, cover, and simmer over medium heat until the greens are tender, about 10 minutes. Add the beans and cook, stirring, until heated through, about 5 minutes. Serve over the rice.

SERVES 4

Hot Salsa Pinto Beans and Rice

∽ Texmati rice, a domestic basmati hybrid, provides a fragrant base for the spicy beans, but most any variety will do. For an even quicker version of this dish, simply combine a jar of prepared salsa with the canned pinto beans in a saucepan, stir over medium heat until heated through, and serve over the rice.

1 tablespoon vegetable oil

½ cup coarsely chopped celery

1 large onion, coarsely chopped

1 green bell pepper, coarsely chopped

2 large garlic cloves, minced

1 (28-ounce) can diced tomatoes, drained

1 ½ cups vegetable stock or water

2 tablespoons tomato paste

½ teaspoon paprika

½ teaspoon salt

¼ teaspoon cayenne

⅛ teaspoon freshly ground black pepper

1 ½ to 2 cups cooked or canned pinto beans, rinsed if canned

2 tablespoons chopped fresh parsley

1 tablespoon tamari or other soy sauce

4 to 6 cups Texmati, Louisiana pecan, or other hot cooked rice

In a large saucepan, heat the oil over medium heat until hot. Add the celery, onion, bell pepper, and garlic and cook, stirring occasionally, until the vegetables are soft, about 5 minutes. Add the tomatoes and stock or water and bring to a simmer. Stir in the tomato paste, paprika, salt, cayenne, and black pepper and reduce the heat to low. Add the pinto beans, parsley, and tamari and simmer for 10 minutes. Serve over the hot rice.

SERVES 4

Three-Mushroom Sauté with Brandy Sauce

୬୨ A PACKAGED rice medley, or one of your own creation, would add a special touch to this elegant sauté.

1 tablespoon olive oil

¼ cup minced onion

1 tablespoon minced carrot

1 tablespoon minced celery

½ teaspoon tomato paste

1 ½ cups water

1 tablespoon tamari or other soy sauce

⅛ teaspoon freshly ground pepper

1 tablespoon cornstarch, dissolved in 1 ½ tablespoons water

4 ounces white mushrooms, trimmed and thinly sliced

4 ounces portobello mushrooms, trimmed and thinly sliced

4 ounces shiitake mushrooms, stemmed and thinly sliced

2 tablespoons brandy

Salt and freshly ground black pepper to taste

4 to 6 cups hot cooked rice medley (packaged or a combination of white, brown, and wild)

Heat 1½ teaspoons of the oil in a medium saucepan over medium heat until hot. Add the onion, carrot, and celery and cook, stirring occasionally, until softened, about 3 minutes. Add the tomato paste, water, tamari, and pepper and cook, stirring frequently, for about 5 minutes, or until the liquid is reduced by one third. Bring to a boil, whisk in the cornstarch mixture, and cook, stirring constantly, until the sauce has thickened, about 2 minutes. Remove from the heat and set aside. Heat the remaining 1½ teaspoons oil in a large skillet over medium-high heat. Add the mushrooms and sauté until the liquid they release has evaporated, about 4 minutes. Add the brandy and cook, stirring, for another 30 seconds. Stir in the sauce and cook until heated through, 3 to 5 minutes. Season to taste with salt and pepper. Serve over the hot cooked rice.

SERVES 4

SOUTHERN FRIED RICE

BLACK-EYED peas and sweet Vidalia onions from Georgia bring a Southern touch to this all-American fried rice.

1 tablespoon olive oil

1 large Vidalia onion, finely chopped

3 cups cold cooked long-grain white or Texmati rice

2 tomatoes, peeled and finely chopped

2 teaspoons fresh lemon juice

1 teaspoon Worcestershire sauce

½ teaspoon Tabasco sauce

½ teaspoon salt

⅛ teaspoon freshly ground black pepper

1½ cups cooked or canned black-eyed peas, rinsed if canned

¼ cup minced fresh parsley

Heat the oil in a large skillet over medium heat until hot. Add the onion and cook until softened, about 5 minutes. Add the rice, tomatoes, lemon juice, Worcestershire, Tabasco, salt, and pepper and stir-fry, breaking up any clumps of rice, for about 5 minutes, or until hot. Stir in the black-eyed peas and parsley and cook, stirring, until the peas are hot. Adjust the seasonings if necessary, and serve.

SERVES 4

SHREDDED VEGGIE RICE

USE either white or brown long-grain rice for this quick and colorful stir-fry made with garden-fresh vegetables. The vegetables can be shredded in a food processor using the shredding disc or with a box grater.

1 tablespoon vegetable oil

1 small onion, shredded

1 large carrot, shredded

1 zucchini, shredded

1 yellow squash, shredded

2 scallions, trimmed and minced

1 large garlic clove, minced

2 teaspoons grated fresh ginger

3 cups cold cooked long-grain white or brown rice

2 tablespoons tamari or other soy sauce

Heat the oil in a large skillet over medium heat until hot. Add the onion, carrot, zucchini, yellow squash, scallions, garlic, and ginger and stir-fry until the vegetables are beginning to soften, about 2 to 4 minutes. Add the rice and tamari and cook, stirring and breaking up any clumps of rice, until the rice is heated through, about 3 minutes. Serve hot.

SERVES 4

ALMOND-RICE BURGERS

〰️ SHORT-GRAIN brown rice holds together well and adds a nutty flavor that complements the almonds in these tasty burgers. Serve on their own with a sauce or chutney, or on burger rolls with all the trimmings.

1 cup cooked short-grain brown rice
¾ cup cooked or canned pinto beans, rinsed if canned
1½ cups dry bread crumbs
½ cup coarsely ground almonds
¼ cup grated onion
¼ cup grated carrots
½ teaspoon paprika
½ teaspoon salt
⅛ teaspoon cayenne
2 tablespoons vegetable oil

In a large bowl, combine the rice, beans, ½ cup of the bread crumbs, the almonds, onion, carrots, paprika, salt, and cayenne and stir until well blended or combine in a food processor and process until blended. Shape the mixture into six ¼-inch-thick patties. Spread the remaining 1 cup bread crumbs on a plate and coat the patties on both sides. Heat the oil in a large skillet over medium-high heat until hot. Add the patties and cook for about 3 minutes per side, until golden brown. Serve immediately.

SERVES 6

Barbecued Tofu over Rice

ᏜᏗ TOFU readily soaks up this rich homemade barbecue sauce. Long-grain white rice would be more traditional, but I prefer a fragrant jasmine, to complement the sweetness of the sauce.

1 small onion, coarsely chopped

1 large garlic clove, coarsely chopped

1 cup tomato sauce

2 tablespoons fresh lemon juice

1 tablespoon Worcestershire sauce

2 teaspoons Dijon mustard

2 to 3 tablespoons brown sugar

½ teaspoon salt

¼ teaspoon cayenne

1 tablespoon vegetable oil

1 pound extra-firm tofu, drained, patted dry, and
*   cut into ½-inch-wide slices*

4 to 6 cups hot cooked jasmine or long-grain white
*   or brown rice*

Place the onion and garlic in a food processor and pulse until the onion is finely chopped. Add the tomato sauce, lemon juice, Worcestershire sauce, mustard, sugar, salt, and cayenne and process until smooth. Transfer the sauce mixture to a saucepan, bring to a simmer, and simmer gently, stirring occasionally, for about 30 minutes, until slightly thickened. Remove from the heat. Heat the oil in a large skillet over medium-high heat until hot. Add the tofu slices, in batches, turning once, and cook until golden brown, about 3 minutes on each side. Add the barbecue sauce to the tofu, bring to a simmer, and simmer for about 10 minutes, spooning the sauce over the tofu to coat well. Serve over the hot rice.

SERVES 4

Asparagus and Wild Rice Medley with Herbed Mushroom Sauce

ꙮ PUREEING tender mushrooms and white beans with vegetable stock makes a rich, velvety sauce that coats the flavorful rice medley in this dish. It's a great way to stretch a small amount of leftover wild rice. If vegetable stock is unavailable, substitute 2 vegetable bouillon cubes or 2 teaspoons of granules, dissolved in 2 cups of hot water.

2 cups vegetable stock or water

8 ounces mushrooms, trimmed and halved

½ cup cooked or canned Great Northern beans, rinsed if canned

2 tablespoons tamari or other soy sauce

1 tablespoon minced fresh parsley

1 teaspoon minced fresh thyme or ¼ teaspoon dried

Salt and freshly ground black pepper to taste

2 cups cooked long-grain white rice

2 cups cooked long-grain brown rice

1 cup cooked wild rice

8 ounces thin asparagus, trimmed and cut diagonally into 1-inch pieces

Place the stock or water and mushrooms in a medium saucepan and bring to a boil. Reduce the heat to medium and simmer until the mushrooms soften, about 5 minutes. Transfer the mushroom mixture to a blender, add the beans, tamari, parsley, thyme, and salt and pepper, and puree. Return the mixture to the saucepan, taste, and adjust the seasoning; keep warm. Meanwhile, combine all the rice in a large non-stick skillet and heat over medium heat, stirring occasionally, until hot. While the rice is heating, place the asparagus in a vegetable steamer and steam over boiling water for 3 to 5 minutes, or until tender. Divide the rice medley among four serving bowls and top with the sauce. Distribute the asparagus over the top and serve.

SERVES 4

Rice-Stuffed Summer Squash

෨෨ THE nutty flavor and cohesive texture of short-grain brown rice work well in this stuffing. Zucchini can be substituted for the yellow squash, or use two of each squash.

4 yellow squash, halved lengthwise and seeded
2 cups cooked short-grain brown, jasmine, or other rice
2 tablespoons minced onion
2 tablespoons minced green bell pepper
2 tablespoons minced fresh parsley
½ cup silken tofu
3 tablespoons freshly grated Parmesan cheese (or soy cheese)
¼ teaspoon salt
⅛ teaspoon cayenne

Bring a large pot of water to a boil, add the squash halves, and blanch for 1 to 2 minutes. Drain and set aside. Preheat the oven to 350°F. Lightly oil a large baking dish. In a large bowl, combine the rice, onion, green pepper, parsley, tofu, cheese, salt, and cayenne, mixing well. Spoon the stuffing into the squash halves and arrange them in the baking dish. Bake until the squash is tender and the stuffing is lightly browned, about 30 minutes. Serve hot.

SERVES 4

Succotash Sauté

O N E taste will tell you that corn and lima beans were meant to be combined with rice. Sweet bits of red bell pepper add color, texture, and flavor to this simple sauté, which can be made with any variety of long-grain rice.

1 tablespoon vegetable oil
2 scallions, trimmed and minced
¼ cup chopped red bell pepper
4 cups cooked long-grain white, Texmati, or other rice
1 (10-ounce) package frozen succotash, cooked according to
    the package instructions
1 tablespoon minced fresh parsley
½ teaspoon salt
⅛ teaspoon freshly ground black pepper

Heat the oil in a large skillet over medium-high heat until hot. Add the scallions and red pepper and cook, stirring, for 1 minute, or until slightly softened. Add the rice, succotash, parsley, salt, and pepper and cook, stirring occasionally, for about 6 to 8 minutes, or until heated through. Serve hot.

SERVES 4

Orange-Glazed Tofu Strips over Rice

ᑭᑫ ADDITIONAL orange juice can be substituted for the Grand Marnier in this tasty sauce. I recommend flavorful brown Texmati or Louisiana pecan rice, but feel free to experiment.

1 tablespoon vegetable oil

1 pound extra-firm tofu, drained, and cut into 1/4-inch-wide strips

Salt and freshly ground black pepper to taste

½ cup fresh orange juice

¼ cup Grand Marnier or other orange liqueur

1 garlic clove, minced

¼ cup golden raisins

1½ tablespoons tomato paste

1 tablespoon Dijon mustard

1 teaspoon sugar

½ cup water

1 tablespoon cornstarch dissolved in 1 tablespoon water

1 teaspoon fresh lemon juice

4 to 6 cups hot cooked brown Texmati, Louisiana pecan, or other rice

Heat the oil in a large skillet over medium-high heat until hot. Add the tofu and sauté until golden brown, about 5 minutes. Season with salt and pepper, remove from the heat, and set aside in the skillet. In a small saucepan, combine the orange juice, liqueur, garlic, and raisins and bring to a boil. Reduce the heat to medium, stir in the tomato paste, mustard, sugar, and water, and simmer for 5 minutes or until slightly syrupy. Stir in cornstarch mixture, stirring to thicken, about 1 minute. Add the lemon juice. Pour the sauce over the tofu and simmer until the tofu is heated through and glazed with sauce, about 5 minutes. Serve over the hot rice.

SERVES 4

RICE AND VEGETABLE HASH

⌒⌒ THIS is the perfect recipe for leftover potatoes and rice. Short-grain brown rice works best in this stick-to-your-ribs dish. Serve it with ketchup, of course.

1 tablespoon vegetable oil

1 large Vidalia or other sweet onion, chopped

1 red bell pepper, chopped

1 carrot, shredded

1 pound Yukon gold or other potatoes, cooked, cooled,
    and cut into ¼-inch dice

2 cups cooked short-grain brown rice

1 tablespoon tamari or other soy sauce

½ teaspoon salt

⅛ teaspoon freshly ground black pepper

Heat the oil in a large skillet over medium heat until hot. Add the onion, bell pepper, and carrot and cook, stirring occasionally, until soft, about 5 minutes. Add the potatoes and cook, stirring frequently, until lightly browned, about 3 to 5 minutes. Add the rice, tamari, salt, and pepper and cook for about 5 minutes, or until heated through. Serve hot.

SERVES 4

Cumin-Spiced Red Beans and Rice

CUMIN, cilantro, and jalapeños add a decidedly Southwestern accent to this Southern favorite. For a variation, add a can of diced tomatoes along with the beans.

1 tablespoon vegetable oil
1 small onion, finely minced
1 small green bell pepper, chopped
1 or 2 jalapeño chiles, seeded and minced
½ cup chopped celery
2 large garlic cloves, minced
1 teaspoon ground cumin
½ teaspoon paprika
¼ teaspoon dried oregano
½ teaspoon salt, or to taste
⅛ teaspoon cayenne, or to taste
⅛ teaspoon freshly ground black pepper, or to taste
3 cups cooked or canned red beans (kidney, adzuki, or
    pinto beans can be substituted), rinsed if canned
4 cups hot cooked Texmati, Louisiana pecan, or long-grain rice
2 tablespoons minced fresh cilantro, for garnish

Heat the oil in a large skillet over medium heat until hot. Add the onion, bell pepper, jalapeños, celery, garlic, cumin, paprika, oregano, salt, cayenne, and black pepper and cook, stirring occasionally, until the vegetables are softened and lightly browned, about 10 minutes. Add the beans and cook 10 minutes longer, stirring occasionally, to allow the flavors to blend. Taste and adjust the seasoning. Serve the beans on top of the rice, sprinkled with the cilantro.

SERVES 4 TO 6

HOPPIN' JOHN WITH COLLARDS

HOPPIN' JOHN is a traditional Southern dish of rice and black-eyed peas, said to bring good luck for the New Year. It's typically served with collard greens on the side; I prefer to add them to the Hoppin' John for a nutritious one-dish meal. If collards are unavailable, kale or another dark leafy green can be substituted.

1 pound collard greens, trimmed
1 tablespoon olive oil
1 onion, chopped
1 ½ cups cooked or canned black-eyed peas, rinsed if canned
3 cups cooked long-grain white rice
½ teaspoon salt
⅛ teaspoon freshly ground black pepper
Tabasco sauce to taste

Cook the collard greens in a large pot of boiling salted water for 3 to 5 minutes, until just tender, then rinse under cool water and drain well. Coarsely chop and set aside. Heat the oil in a large skillet over medium-high heat until hot. Add the onion and cook for 5 minutes, or until soft. Add the black-eyed peas, rice, and collards, and cook, stirring occasionally, for 5 minutes, or until heated through. Season with the salt and pepper and a splash of Tabasco and serve.

SERVES 4

Rice and Cabbage with Apples and Raisins

C&O THIS delicious recipe offers interesting variations. For an Eastern European accent, omit the cinnamon and add caraway seeds. For a taste of India, stir some curry powder into the cabbage and onion.

1 tablespoon vegetable oil
½ cup minced onion
2 cups shredded green cabbage
1 ¼ cups basmati rice (or rice of your choice)
1 Granny Smith apple, diced
2 tablespoons golden raisins
2 cups water
½ teaspoon ground cinnamon
Salt and freshly ground black pepper to taste

Heat the oil in a large saucepan over medium heat until hot. Add the onion and cabbage and cook, stirring occasionally, until softened, about 5 minutes. Stir in the rice, apple, and raisins and cook for 1 minute. Stir in the water and cinnamon and bring to a boil over high heat. Reduce the heat to low, cover, and simmer until all the liquid is absorbed and the rice is tender, about 20 to 25 minutes. Season to taste with salt and pepper and serve.

SERVES 4

Quick Veggie Chili over Texmati Rice

෨ TRY one of the rices from the Lundberg Family Farm in this zesty chili: Texmati, their basmati hybrid, or Wehani, a mellow brown rice, are both good choices, each adding its own particular nuance. If you put the rice on to cook as you begin to assemble the chili ingredients, everything should be ready at the same time.

1 ½ cups Texmati or Wehani rice
Salt
1 tablespoon olive oil
1 onion, minced
1 green bell pepper, minced
1 garlic clove, minced
3 tablespoons chili powder, or more to taste
2 tablespoons tomato paste
1 ½ cups water
3 cups cooked or canned pinto beans, rinsed if canned
1 (16-ounce) can diced tomatoes
1 cup tomato puree
Freshly ground black pepper to taste

In a medium saucepan, combine the rice, 3 cups water, and ½ teaspoon salt and bring to a boil. Reduce the heat, cover, and simmer for 20 to 40 minutes (depending on the type of rice), until the rice is tender. Remove from the heat. While the rice is cooking, heat the oil in a large skillet over low heat until hot. Add the onion, bell pepper, garlic, and chili powder and cook, covered, for 5 minutes, or until the vegetables are tender. Remove the cover, stir in the tomato paste, add the water, pinto beans, tomatoes, tomato puree, and salt and pepper to taste, and cook for 20 minutes, or until the desired consistency is reached. Serve over the hot rice.

SERVES 4

Rice with Sage-Infused White Bean Sauce

GO FRESH sage and white beans are a classic Italian combination. Here the dusky flavor of the herb permeates a delicate white bean sauce. Try it on a rice medley—it goes especially well with the slightly nutty flavors of long-grain brown and wild rice.

2 tablespoons olive oil
1 carrot, finely chopped
1 onion, minced
1 garlic clove, minced
1 tablespoon chopped fresh sage or 1 teaspoon dried
1½ cups cooked or canned Great Northern beans or
    other white beans, rinsed if canned
2 to 3 cups vegetable stock
Salt and freshly ground black pepper to taste
4 to 6 cups hot cooked rice medley
    (packaged or a combination of your choice)
2 tablespoons chopped fresh parsley, for garnish

In a large saucepan, heat the oil over low heat until hot. Add the carrot, onion, garlic, and sage and sauté until the onion is soft, about 5 minutes. Add the beans and 2 cups stock, bring to a simmer, and simmer for about 20 minutes, or until the liquid reduces slightly and the vegetables are very soft. Transfer the bean mixture to a food processor and puree until almost smooth. Transfer the bean puree to a saucepan, season with salt and pepper, and stir in up to 1 cup more stock to make a smooth, thick sauce. Reheat the sauce over low heat and serve over the hot rice, sprinkled with the parsley.

SERVES 4

Vegetable Etouffée

⟲ ONE of my favorite ways to enjoy rice is topped with the famous Cajun stew called *étouffée*, which translates from the French as "smothered." Although there are many variations on this classic dish, étouffée is usually made with crawfish or shrimp. This brimming-with-vegetables version still has that great New Orleans taste because it's based on a dark roux, the traditional butter-and-flour thickener (although olive oil stands in for butter here) and the famous Cajun "trinity" of onion, celery, and bell pepper. The ingredients list may seem long, but this stew cooks in only 30 minutes.

¼ cup all-purpose flour
1½ tablespoons olive oil
1 onion, finely chopped
1 celery rib, finely chopped
1 green bell pepper, finely chopped
2 zucchini, halved lengthwise and cut
    into ½-inch slices
2 garlic cloves, minced
2 cups water
1 (16-ounce) can tomato puree
1 teaspoon dried thyme
1 teaspoon filé powder
1 bay leaf
Salt and freshly ground black pepper to taste
¼ teaspoon cayenne
1½ cups cooked or canned kidney beans, rinsed
    if canned
3 scallions, trimmed and chopped
2 tablespoons minced fresh parsley
Hot pepper sauce to taste (optional)
4 to 6 cups hot cooked long-grain white,
    Louisiana pecan, or other rice

Heat a large skillet over medium heat. Add the flour and stir constantly until it turns light brown, about 3 to 5 minutes; do not let burn. Transfer the flour to a small plate and set aside. Heat the oil in the same skillet over medium heat. Add the onion, celery, bell pepper, zucchini, and garlic, cover, and cook for 5 to 7 minutes, or until soft. Add the browned flour, stirring to coat the vegetables. Add the water, tomato puree, thyme, filé powder, bay leaf, salt and pepper, and cayenne, bring to a simmer, and simmer over low heat for 10 minutes, stirring occasionally, until thickened. Add the beans, scallions, and parsley and cook for 5 minutes longer, or until heated through. Taste and adjust the seasoning, adding a splash of hot pepper sauce if desired. Serve over the hot rice.

SERVES 4

RICETERA...

A PILAF BY ANY OTHER NAME

Perloo, pilaf, pilav, pulao, pulau, polo — all words that mean the same thing in different parts of the world, from the American South to the Middle East. Any way you pronounce it, it's a dish made by sautéing rice in oil or butter and then slow-cooking it with a combination of other ingredients.

CHAPTER 6

Hearty Soups

Rice is a natural addition to soup. Rice gives it substance and texture and amplifies the flavors of the surrounding broth. The soups in this chapter, such as Okra Gumbo, Minestrone, and Indonesian Peanut Soup, are a selection of global delights that feature rice as a major component, making them hearty enough to serve as one-dish meals.

Long-grain rice is generally added to broth-based soups, as the distinct grains retain their shape among the vegetables and other ingredients. However, short-grain rice cooked until soft can be used to enrich and thicken cream soups.

I keep small portions of cooked rice in the freezer, ready for a quick addition to a vegetable soup when the mood strikes. Add some warm bread or rolls, and dinner is served.

OKRA GUMBO

∽ SINCE *gumbo* is actually an African word for *okra*, the name of this recipe may seem redundant. But with a hearty soup this delicious, why mince words? Be sure to place a bottle of Tabasco sauce on the table so your guests can spice up their gumbo to their liking. Although some versions of gumbo are made with just a small amount of rice, I prefer it thick with rice and served as a more substantial stew-like dish.

1 tablespoon olive oil

1 onion, diced

1 green bell pepper, diced

½ cup chopped celery

2 garlic cloves, minced

6 cups water

1 (16-ounce) can diced tomatoes

1½ cups sliced fresh or frozen okra

1 teaspoon filé powder

1 teaspoon dried thyme

1 teaspoon salt, or to taste

¼ teaspoon freshly ground black pepper, or to taste

⅛ teaspoon cayenne

1½ cups cooked or canned kidney beans, rinsed if canned

3 to 4 cups hot cooked white, Texmati, or other long-grain rice

Heat the oil in a large saucepan over medium heat until hot. Add the onion, bell pepper, celery, and garlic, cover, and cook, stirring occasionally, for 5 minutes, or until soft. Remove the cover, add the water, tomatoes, okra, filé powder, thyme, salt, black pepper, and cayenne, and bring to a simmer. Simmer over low heat, stirring occasionally, for 30 minutes. Add the kidney beans and simmer 5 to 10 minutes longer to heat through. Taste and adjust the seasoning. To serve, place the rice in soup bowls and ladle the hot gumbo over it.

SERVES 4 TO 6

THYME-SCENTED MUSHROOM-RICE SOUP

෨෨ OVERFLOWING with juicy mushroom slices, this soup has a rich, complex flavor that belies its ease of preparation.

1 tablespoon olive oil

2 ~~leeks, white part only,~~ *onions* chopped

(1 celery rib, including leaves, chopped)

1 cup long-grain white rice *— used brn basmati*

5 cups vegetable stock or water *— could do 6 cups — otherwise its almost moreskw (5 is okay, just light on broth) just light on*

(2 tablespoons dry white wine)

1 tablespoon minced fresh thyme or 1 teaspoon dried

~~2~~ ✗ bay leaf

3 cups sliced white button mushrooms *— 2 10 oz containers*

2 tablespoons minced fresh parsley

Salt and freshly ground black pepper to taste

Heat the oil in a large saucepan over medium heat until hot. Add the leeks and celery and cook, stirring occasionally, until softened, about 5 minutes. Add the rice, stock or water, wine (the dried thyme) if using, and the bay leaf, bring to a simmer, and simmer for 15 minutes. Stir in the mushrooms, parsley, and the fresh thyme, if using. Season with salt and pepper to taste and cook for 10 minutes longer, or until the rice is tender. Serve hot.

SERVES 4

Minestrone with Rice

୬୬ I USUALLY use Wehani for its deep flavor, or a short-grain brown rice for its chewy texture in this hearty soup, but you can use any variety of rice. Adding rice to minestrone makes a nice change from pasta.

1 tablespoon olive oil

1 onion, minced

2 carrots, diced

2 garlic cloves, minced

8 ounces green beans, trimmed and cut into 2-inch pieces

1 (16-ounce) can diced tomatoes

8 cups water

1 bay leaf

1 tablespoon minced fresh basil or 1 teaspoon dried

1 teaspoon minced fresh oregano or ¼ teaspoon dried

½ teaspoon minced fresh thyme or ⅛ teaspoon dried

2 zucchini, diced

1½ to 2 cups cooked or canned cannellini beans, rinsed if canned

1 teaspoon salt

⅛ teaspoon freshly ground black pepper

1½ cups cooked short-grain brown, Wehani, or other rice

¼ cup minced fresh parsley

Heat the oil in a large stockpot over medium heat until hot. Add the onion, carrots, and garlic and cook, stirring frequently, for about 5 minutes, or until the vegetables begin to soften. Add the green beans, tomatoes, water, bay leaf, and the dried basil, oregano, and thyme, if using, and bring to a boil.

Reduce the heat and simmer for 30 minutes or until the liquid reduces slightly and the vegetables are soft. Add the zucchini, cannellini beans, salt, and pepper and simmer for 10 minutes. Adjust the seasonings and remove the bay leaf. Stir in the cooked rice, parsley, and the fresh basil, oregano, and thyme, if using, heat through, and ladle into bowls.

SERVES 6 TO 8

SHIITAKE MISO SOUP

MISO is a rich Japanese soybean paste that is said to have many healing properties. Be sure not to boil the soup once the miso paste has been added, since boiling destroys valuable enzymes. Long- or short-grain brown rice would be a good choice here for maximum nutritional benefits.

5 cups water
1 cup sliced stemmed shiitake mushrooms
½ cup chopped scallions
¼ cup finely shredded carrots
½ teaspoon minced fresh ginger
1 tablespoon tamari or other soy sauce
3 tablespoons miso paste
1 cup chopped fresh spinach leaves
1 cup cooked long- or short-grain brown rice
4 ounces firm silken tofu, drained, patted dry, and diced

Bring the water to a boil in a medium saucepan over high heat. Add the mushrooms, scallions, carrots, ginger, and tamari, reduce the heat to medium, and simmer for 10 minutes, or until the vegetables soften. Reduce the heat to low. Transfer about ¼ cup of the hot soup to a small bowl and add the miso paste, blending well. Stir the blended miso into the soup along with the chopped spinach and simmer for 2 minutes, being careful not to boil. Divide the rice and tofu among four soup bowls and ladle the hot soup into the bowls.

SERVES 4

Indonesian Peanut Soup

◯◯ PEANUT BUTTER and coconut milk blend harmoniously with ginger, lime juice, and chiles in a sublime soup made substantial with the last-minute addition of cooked rice. A fragrant jasmine or basmati would complement the delightful flavor and aroma of this soup. Kechap manis, a sweet, thick soy sauce, is available at Asian markets.

1 tablespoon peanut oil

1 onion, chopped

1 red bell pepper, chopped

2 garlic cloves, minced

1 small hot chile, seeded and minced

1 tablespoon minced fresh ginger

½ cup chunky peanut butter

1 cup unsweetened coconut milk

2 tablespoons kechap manis

1 tablespoon fresh lime juice

4 cups water

2 cups cooked rice, preferably basmati or jasmine

Salt and freshly ground black pepper to taste

¼ cup chopped peanuts, for garnish

Heat the oil in a large saucepan over medium heat until hot. Add the onion, bell pepper, garlic, chile, and ginger and cook, stirring occasionally, until soft, about 5 minutes. One at a time, stir in the peanut butter, coconut milk, kechap manis, lime juice, and water, blending well after each addition. Bring to a simmer and simmer for 15 to 20 minutes, until the vegetables are tender and the flavors are well blended. Reduce the heat to low, add the rice, and season to taste with salt and pepper. Simmer for 5 minutes or until heated through. To serve, ladle the soup into bowls and sprinkle with the chopped peanuts.

SERVES 4

VEGETABLE RICE SOUP

HOMEMADE vegetable soup in less than 30 minutes? I put this soup together when I'm short on time and ingredients but crave a vegetable soup with a rich simmered-for-hours flavor. I use whatever rice I happen to have on hand—leftover wild rice medley is especially tasty. Add a cup of cooked beans for additional substance and protein.

1 tablespoon olive oil
1 large onion, chopped
2 carrots, chopped
½ cup chopped celery
1 garlic clove, minced
6 cups water
2 tablespoons tamari or other soy sauce
2 teaspoons vegetable bouillon granules or 2 bouillon cubes
1 cup frozen peas
Salt and freshly ground black pepper to taste
2 cups cooked rice
1 tablespoon minced fresh parsley, for garnish

Heat the oil in a large saucepan over medium heat until hot. Add the onion, carrots, celery, and garlic, cover, and cook, stirring occasionally, until softened, about 5 minutes. Add the water, tamari, and vegetable bouillon and bring to a simmer, then reduce the heat to low and simmer, until the vegetables are tender, about 15 minutes. Add the peas and salt and pepper to taste and gently cook 5 minutes longer. Stir in the rice and heat through, then ladle into bowls. Garnish with the parsley.

SERVES 4 TO 6

"Rice and Hot" Thai Soup

DELICATE grains of jasmine rice absorb this flavorful broth, hot with chiles and tangy with lemongrass, ginger, and lime juice.

6 cups water

1 teaspoon salt

3 lemongrass stalks, cut into 1-inch lengths

2 serrano chiles, thinly sliced

1 teaspoon slivered fresh ginger

1 cup canned sliced bamboo shoots, drained and rinsed

½ cup unsweetened coconut milk

1 tablespoon tamari or other soy sauce

Juice of 1 lime

3 cups cooked jasmine rice

¼ cup coarsely chopped fresh Thai basil, for garnish

In a large saucepan, combine the water, salt, lemongrass, chiles, and ginger. Bring to a boil, then reduce the heat and simmer for 20 minutes. Strain the broth through a sieve, return it to the saucepan, and boil for 2 minutes. Reduce the heat to low and add the bamboo shoots, coconut milk, tamari, and lime juice. Stir well and simmer for 5 minutes. Place ½ cup of rice in the bottom of each bowl, ladle the soup over the rice, sprinkle with the basil leaves, and serve.

SERVES 6

CREAMY WINTER VEGETABLE SOUP

〰 RICE is used to thicken as well as to enrich this warming winter soup. Very soft rice works best, so if your cooked rice is on the firm side, add it to the pot as the vegetables are simmering to cook it a little longer.

1 tablespoon olive oil
1 onion, diced
1 carrot, chopped
¼ cup minced celery
1 Yukon Gold or other potato, peeled and diced
1 cup diced butternut squash
1 garlic clove, minced
½ teaspoon dried marjoram
5 cups water
2 cups cooked white rice
Salt and freshly ground black pepper to taste
Minced fresh parsley or chives, for garnish

Heat the oil in a large saucepan over medium heat until hot. Add the onion, carrot, and celery and cook, covered, for 5 minutes, or until softened. Add the potato, squash, garlic, marjoram, and water, bring to a simmer, and simmer for 20 minutes, or until the vegetables are tender. Stir in the cooked rice and remove from the heat. Puree the soup mixture, in batches, in a food processor until smooth and return to the saucepan. Reheat slowly over low heat, stirring occasionally. Season with salt and pepper to taste and serve sprinkled with the parsley or chives.

SERVES 6

White and Wild Watercress Soup

WILD rice and woodsy mushrooms are a natural combination, and the touch of thyme enhances the rich flavors in this simple but elegant soup. The watercress is added near the end of the cooking time so it retains its fresh taste and vivid color.

1 tablespoon vegetable oil

1 onion, minced

2 celery ribs, minced

1 cup wild rice

8 cups vegetable stock or water

1 teaspoon salt

⅛ teaspoon cayenne

1 tablespoon chopped fresh thyme or 1 teaspoon dried

1 bay leaf

1 cup long-grain white rice

1 cup diced mushrooms, preferably shiitake (stemmed), cremini,
*   or other exotic mushrooms*

2 bunches watercress, chopped (tough stems removed)

Heat the oil in a large saucepan over medium heat until hot. Add the onion and celery and cook until softened, about 5 minutes. Stir in the wild rice, add the stock or water, salt, and cayenne, and bring to a boil. Reduce the heat to low, add the dried thyme, if using, and the bay leaf, cover, and simmer for 20 minutes. Add the white rice and mushrooms and simmer for 20 minutes longer. Stir in the watercress and the fresh thyme, if using, and cook 5 minutes longer, or until the rice is tender. Taste and adjust the seasoning, discard the bay leaf, and serve.

SERVES 6 TO 8

SENEGALESE-STYLE CURRIED SOUP

∽ INSPIRED by the classic curried soups of Senegal, this uses rice both as a thickener and to mellow out the flavorful seasonings. Garnish with chopped peanuts or golden raisins.

1 tablespoon vegetable oil
1 large onion, chopped
½ cup chopped celery
1 Granny Smith apple, peeled and chopped
1½ tablespoons curry powder
½ teaspoon salt
¼ teaspoon cayenne
About 4 cups vegetable stock or water
1½ cups cooked long- or short-grain white rice
Chopped peanuts or raisins, for garnish

Heat the oil in a large saucepan over medium heat until hot. Add the onion and celery and cook for 5 minutes, or until the vegetables are soft. Stir in the apple, curry powder, salt, cayenne, and 3½ cups of the stock or water and bring to a boil. Add the rice and simmer, stirring occasionally, for 15 minutes, or until the rice is very soft. Transfer the soup to a food processor, in batches if necessary, and puree. Pour into a large bowl and whisk in as much of the remaining stock or water as necessary to achieve the desired consistency. Refrigerate for 2 hours, or until cold. Serve the soup chilled, garnished with peanuts or raisins.

SERVES 4

RICETERA...
RICE IN MANY GUISES

RICE IS USED to make a number of other food products.
Here is a list of some of them:

Toasted or puffed breakfast cereals
Rice cakes (made from puffed rice)
Vinegar
Sake and other wines
Cooking wines (mirin)
Beer
Tea (Japanese: genmai cha; *Chinese:* sao my cha)
Crackers
Noodles
Flour (especially for foods for those with wheat allergies)
Candies
Wrappers (used to make spring rolls)
Rice bran oil

CHAPTER 7

Main-Dish Salads

Rice was made for main-dish salads. Long-grain rice, with its distinct separate grains, is especially suited to salads because it retains its shape and texture when combined with other ingredients. In addition, the light, fluffy grains readily absorb flavorful dressings and other flavors.

Rice adds a wholesome goodness to salads, especially when combined with beans and a variety of vegetables, making them satisfying and nutritious meals in themselves. Among the delectable offerings in this chapter are Black Bean and Avocado Rice Salad, Double Mango Rice Salad, and Cannellini Beans and Rice with Lemon-Tarragon Vinaigrette.

Cold cooked rice works best, and most rice salads benefit from an opportunity to rest for at least an hour before serving to allow the flavors to reach their peak. This quality makes them perfect for make-ahead suppers on hot summer nights or easy take-along food for a picnic.

MEDITERRANEAN RICE SALAD
WITH ROASTED RED PEPPERS

GARLIC, fresh herbs, and roasted red peppers imbue this salad with full-bodied Mediterranean flavors. Use jarred roasted red peppers packed in oil for ease of preparation. Grated fennel adds a slightly sweet taste and a fresh-tasting crunch.

2 tablespoons balsamic vinegar
2 tablespoons fresh lemon juice
2 garlic cloves, minced
1 tablespoon minced fresh basil or 1 teaspoon dried
½ teaspoon minced fresh oregano or ⅛ teaspoon dried
½ teaspoon salt
⅛ teaspoon freshly ground black pepper
⅓ cup olive oil
3 cups cold cooked brown basmati or other rice
½ cup grated fennel
½ cup chopped red onion
1 cup cooked or canned chickpeas, rinsed if canned
1 (4-ounce) jar roasted red peppers, drained and chopped
Salad greens, for serving
Oil-cured black olives, pitted, for garnish

In a small bowl, whisk together the vinegar, lemon juice, garlic, basil, oregano, salt, and pepper. Whisk in the oil in a slow, steady stream until emulsified and smooth; set aside. In a large bowl, combine the rice, fennel, onion, chickpeas, and roasted red peppers. Add the dressing and toss well. Cover and refrigerate for at least 30 minutes before serving. Line a platter with salad greens and top with the rice salad. Garnish with the black olives and serve.

SERVES 4

BLACK BEAN AND AVOCADO RICE SALAD

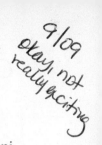

❧ A BASKET of warm corn bread would make a good accompaniment for this south-of-the-border salad. Choose long-grain white rice for a striking color contrast or brown rice to add a slightly nutty flavor to the dish.

1 teaspoon minced lime zest

3 tablespoons fresh lime juice

1 tablespoon cider vinegar

2 tablespoons fresh orange juice

½ teaspoon minced garlic

1 teaspoon light brown sugar

½ teaspoon chili powder

½ teaspoon salt

⅛ teaspoon cayenne

⅓ cup olive oil

2 avocados

1 tablespoon fresh lemon juice

3 cups cold cooked long-grain white or brown rice

1½ cups cooked or canned black beans, rinsed if canned

½ red onion, chopped

1 (4-ounce) can minced jalapeño chiles

Torn romaine lettuce leaves, for serving

12 cherry tomatoes, halved, for garnish

In a small bowl, whisk together the lime zest, lime juice, vinegar, orange juice, garlic, brown sugar, chili powder, salt, and cayenne. Whisk in the oil in a slow, steady stream until emulsified and smooth; set aside. Peel and pit the avocados, cut into ½-inch dice, and toss with the lemon juice. In a large bowl, combine the rice, beans, onion, jalapeños, and avocados. Add the dressing and toss gently to combine. Line plates or shallow bowls with lettuce and top with the salad. Garnish with the cherry tomatoes and serve.

SERVES 4

ORANGE-SCENTED
BROCCOLI-RICE SALAD

A REFRESHING touch of orange enlivens this vibrant salad. Broccoli boosts the vitamin C content and adds calcium, for a light lunch that is as healthful as it is delicious. Loaves of pita bread spread with hummus would make a nice accompaniment.

2 large garlic cloves

← 1 shallot

1 tablespoon grated orange zest — lemon zest

3 tablespoons fresh orange juice

3 tablespoons white ~red~ wine vinegar

1 tablespoon minced fresh parsley ← mint - several tblspns

(½ teaspoon salt)

⅓ cup olive oil

3 cups broccoli flowerets

3 cups cold cooked basmati rice

2 large ripe tomatoes, seeded and diced

1 red bell pepper, chopped

¼ cup minced fresh basil, plus additional whole leaves for garnish)

[Lettuce leaves, for serving)

In a food processor with the machine on, add the garlic and shallot through the feed tube and mince. Add the orange zest, orange juice, vinegar, parsley, and salt and process to blend. With the machine running, add the oil in a slow, steady stream, processing until emulsified and smooth. Set aside. Steam the broccoli over boiling water just until tender, 3 to 5 minutes. In a large bowl, combine the rice, tomatoes, bell pepper, broccoli, and minced basil. Toss gently with the dressing. To serve, line a platter or individual plates with lettuce leaves and mound the salad on top. Garnish with basil leaves.

SERVES 4

Marinated Artichoke and Mushroom Rice Salad

only good for 2 days

eh 6/2013 ~~not bad~~ decent vehicle for marinated artichoke hearts - might buy marinated mushrms too, rather than fresh. else add more sauce from artichoke jar from Trader Joes

THE bold piquancy of artichoke hearts and capers stands out in this Mediterranean-inspired salad. For extra protein, add a can of your favorite beans.

1 (10-ounce) jar marinated artichoke hearts, drained and quartered
1 cup quartered small white mushrooms
1 tablespoon capers, rinsed and drained
½ teaspoon salt
⅛ teaspoon cayenne
⅓ cup olive oil
3 tablespoons fresh lemon juice
4 cups cold cooked long-grain rice (a medley with exotics is nice)
Salad greens, for serving
Cherry tomatoes, for garnish
Oil-cured black olives, for garnish

In a medium bowl, combine the artichoke hearts, mushrooms, capers, salt, cayenne, olive oil, and lemon juice. Add the rice and toss gently to combine. Allow the salad to stand for at least 30 minutes at room temperature for the flavors to develop. Serve on salad greens, garnished with cherry tomatoes and olives.

SERVES 4

DOUBLE MANGO RICE SALAD

∾ BRIGHT, juicy mangoes and mango chutney add a touch of sweetness to this colorful salad. Basmati rice echoes the Indian flavors of the chutney.

*Omit
since use
Trader Joes
mango ginger
chutney*

*before cook
1c*

in chutney

chives ~

½ cup chopped mango chutney

3 tablespoons fresh lime juice

1 teaspoon light brown sugar

⅛ teaspoon ground allspice

⅛ teaspoon cayenne, or to taste

(Salt to taste)

3 cups cold cooked basmati rice *or brown rice – nice! crunch*

1 large mango, peeled, seeded, and cut into ½-inch dice,

  plus mango slices for garnish

1 red bell pepper, cut into ½-inch dice

½ cup minced celery

¼ cup golden raisins

2 tablespoons minced scallions

Lettuce leaves, for serving

In a medium bowl, combine the chutney, lime juice, brown sugar, allspice, cayenne, and salt and mix until well blended. Set aside. In a large bowl, combine the rice with the diced mango, bell pepper, celery, raisins, and scallions. Add the dressing to the salad, toss gently, taste, and adjust the seasoning. Line a platter or individual plates with lettuce, mound the salad on top, and garnish with mango slices.

SERVES 4

Grilled Vegetables and Rice Salad

෨෨ I CREATED this salad when I had leftover grilled vegetable bro-
chettes that I'd served over rice. Combining the grilled vegetables and rice
from the refrigerator the next day seemed like a logical solution. The result
was so delicious I now plan ahead when firing up the grill and pile on extra
veggies to use for this salad.

⅓ cup extra-virgin olive oil

3 tablespoons balsamic vinegar

½ teaspoon minced garlic

1 teaspoon minced fresh basil or ½ teaspoon dried

1 teaspoon minced fresh marjoram or ½ teaspoon dried

½ teaspoon salt

⅛ teaspoon freshly ground black pepper

1 large onion, cut crosswise into ¼-inch slices

1 fennel bulb, trimmed and cut lengthwise into ¼-inch slices

1 red bell pepper, halved

2 large portobello mushroom caps

2 small zucchini, halved lengthwise

4 cups cold cooked long-grain rice

Prepare the grill. In a small bowl, whisk together the olive oil, balsamic vinegar, garlic, basil, marjoram, salt, and pepper. Place the vegetables in a single
layer on a baking sheet and spoon the dressing over them, turning to coat.
Grill the vegetables, either directly on the grill rack or using a mesh grill basket, until slightly charred but still firm, about 5 minutes. Reserve any dressing remaining on the baking sheet. Transfer to a platter to cool. Cut the vegetables into ½-inch pieces and place in a large bowl. Add the rice and any
remaining dressing and toss well to combine. Serve with grilled garlic bread.

SERVES 4

Sushi Rice Salad

~~ THERE are many ways to enjoy sushi rice without ever going near a piece of fish, raw or otherwise. Two such preparations are the refreshing rice salads called *chirashi-zushi,* sushi rice topped with vegetables, and *bara-zushi,* which means "scattered sushi." This is my own sushi rice salad, made with Japanese-style glutinous rice.

1 ¼ cups Japanese sticky (glutinous) rice
½ teaspoon salt
2 tablespoons rice vinegar
1 teaspoon sugar
1 cup water
2 tablespoons tamari or other soy sauce
1 teaspoon white miso paste
1 teaspoon mirin
1 cup stemmed and sliced shiitake mushrooms
1 carrot, cut into long shreds
1 cup fresh bean sprouts
1 cup snow peas, trimmed and cut into strips
2 tablespoons chopped scallions
1 teaspoon dark sesame oil

Soak the rice in cold water for 30 minutes; drain. Place the rice, 2½ cups water, and the salt in a medium saucepan, cover, and bring to a boil. Reduce the heat to low and simmer for 15 minutes. Remove from the heat and allow to stand for 5 minutes, then transfer the rice to a shallow bowl and let cool to room temperature. In a small saucepan, heat the rice vinegar with the sugar, stirring to dissolve the sugar. Drizzle the vinegar mixture over the cooled rice. Combine the water, tamari, miso paste, and mirin in a saucepan and bring to a simmer over medium heat, stirring to dissolve the miso. Add the mushrooms and carrot and cook until softened, about 2 minutes. Add the bean sprouts and snow peas and cook about 1 minute longer, or until the snow peas turn bright green. Drain and return to the pan, then add the scallions and sesame oil and toss to coat. Spoon the rice into individual bowls and top with the vegetables. Serve warm or at room temperature.

SERVES 4

BROWN RICE AND ADZUKI BEAN SALAD

T H E combination of brown rice and adzuki beans is a protein-rich mainstay of a macrobiotic diet. Adzuki beans are small red Japanese beans that can be found canned or dried in natural food stores. Whenever I eat this salad, I feel energized by the healthful combination of ingredients.

3 cups cooked long-grain brown rice
1 cup ~~cooked or canned~~ *edamame* adzuki beans, rinsed if canned
1 cucumber, peeled, halved lengthwise, seeded, and diced
¼ cup minced scallions
¼ cup minced fresh parsley
1½ cups coarsely chopped watercress (tough stems removed)
3 tablespoons rice wine vinegar
1 tablespoon tamari or other soy sauce
1 tablespoon fresh lemon juice
1 teaspoon minced fresh ginger
½ teaspoon salt
⅛ teaspoon freshly ground black pepper
3 tablespoons dark sesame oil
2 tablespoons vegetable oil

In a large bowl, combine the rice, beans, cucumber, scallions, parsley, and watercress. In a small bowl, whisk together the vinegar, tamari, lemon juice, ginger, salt, and pepper. One at a time, gradually add both oils in a slow, steady stream, whisking constantly until emulsified and smooth. Pour the dressing over the rice mixture and toss gently to coat the rice. Serve in a shallow bowl lined with lettuce leaves if desired.

S E R V E S 4

WALDORF RICE SALAD

∽ THE surprising crunch of apple and walnuts in this vibrant, luscious dish inspired by the classic Waldorf salad will make this a favorite addition to the buffet table. Fragrant basmati rice lends an extra touch of sweetness.

1 large Red Delicious or Granny Smith apple

2 tablespoons fresh lemon juice

3 cups cold cooked basmati rice

¾ cup raisins

¾ cup finely chopped celery

½ cup chopped walnuts

¼ cup minced scallions

½ cup mayonnaise or soy mayonnaise

1 teaspoon Dijon mustard

2 tablespoons cider vinegar

1 teaspoon sugar

½ teaspoon salt

2 tablespoons vegetable oil

Lettuce leaves, for serving

Cut the apple into ½-inch dice and place in a large bowl. Add the lemon juice and toss to coat. Add the rice, raisins, celery, walnuts, and scallions and set aside. In a small bowl, whisk together the mayonnaise, mustard, vinegar, sugar, and salt. Whisk in the oil in a slow, steady stream, until emulsified and smooth. Add the dressing to the salad and mix gently to combine. Cover the salad and refrigerate for at least 30 minutes before serving. To serve, line a shallow bowl or individual plates with lettuce leaves and mound salad on top.

SERVES 4 TO 6

Cannellini Beans and Rice with Lemon-Tarragon Vinaigrette

ᑫᕝ PUT this fresh-tasting tarragon-kissed salad together in the morning so it's ready for a no-fuss dinner on a hot summer night. It's especially good served with warm focaccia, the savory Italian flatbread. If you prefer another fresh herb to the fragrant tarragon, feel free to use it instead.

½ cup minced onion
½ cup minced celery
1½ to 2 cups cooked or canned cannellini beans, rinsed if canned
2 large ripe tomatoes, seeded and chopped
3 cups cold cooked long-grain rice
1 small garlic clove, minced
¼ cup minced fresh tarragon
2 tablespoons minced fresh parsley
1 teaspoon salt
¼ teaspoon freshly ground black pepper
3 tablespoons fresh lemon juice
2 tablespoons white wine vinegar
¼ teaspoon sugar
½ cup olive oil
Torn mixed greens, for serving

In a large bowl, combine the onion, celery, beans, tomatoes, and rice; set aside. In a food processor, combine the garlic, tarragon, parsley, salt, and pepper and process to mince very fine. Add the lemon juice, vinegar, and sugar. With the machine running, gradually add the olive oil in a slow, steady stream, processing until emulsified and smooth. Add enough of the dressing to the rice mixture to coat, tossing gently to combine. Let stand for 30 minutes. To serve, in a large bowl, toss the greens with the remaining dressing. Place the greens in a large shallow serving bowl and mound the rice salad in the center.

SERVES 6

WILD ABOUT RICE SALAD

༄ THIS salad is a great way to use up leftover wild rice, but we enjoy it so much that I usually keep cooked wild rice in the freezer so I can put it together on a whim. Vary the vegetables according to your own preference and availability. Leftover cooked vegetables also make welcome additions.

3 cups cold cooked long-grain white rice
1 cup cold cooked wild rice
¼ cup cider vinegar
½ teaspoon salt
⅛ teaspoon freshly ground black pepper
½ cup olive oil
1 yellow bell pepper, chopped
½ cup frozen peas, thawed
¼ cup minced scallions
¼ cup minced fresh parsley
Torn mixed lettuces, for serving

Place both rices in a large bowl and set aside. In a small bowl, whisk together the vinegar, salt, and pepper. Add the oil in a slow, steady stream, whisking constantly until emulsified and smooth. Pour the dressing over the rice and toss to coat it with the dressing. Add the bell pepper, peas, scallions, and parsley and toss gently to combine. Taste and adjust the seasoning. Serve on a bed of mixed lettuces.

SERVES 4

CARROT AND RAISIN RICE SALAD WITH CASHEWS

BROWN basmati rice adds substance to this slightly sweet salad, inspired by the popular carrot and raisin combination found at many salad bars.

3 cups cold cooked brown basmati rice
2 large carrots, finely shredded
¾ cup golden raisins
¼ cup chopped scallions
1 tablespoon fresh lemon juice
½ cup fresh orange juice
¼ teaspoon ground cinnamon
¼ teaspoon ground allspice
½ teaspoon salt
⅛ teaspoon freshly ground black pepper
¼ cup vegetable oil
Boston lettuce leaves, for serving
½ cup chopped cashews, for garnish

In a large bowl, combine the rice, carrots, raisins, and scallions; set aside. In a small bowl, whisk together the lemon juice, orange juice, cinnamon, allspice, salt, and pepper. Add the oil in a slow, steady stream, whisking constantly until emulsified and smooth. Pour the dressing over the salad and toss gently to combine. Cover the salad and refrigerate for at least 1 hour before serving. To serve, line a shallow serving bowl with lettuce leaves, mound the salad in the lettuce, and garnish with the chopped cashews.

SERVES 4 TO 6

Three-Bean Rice Salad

You could make a quicker version of this salad using a prepared three-bean salad, but I like the fresher taste offered by assembling my own, using just-cooked green beans. If fresh wax beans are in season, you could substitute them for the chickpeas.

8 ounces green beans, cut into 1-inch pieces
1 cup cooked or canned kidney beans, rinsed if canned
1 cup cooked or canned chickpeas, rinsed if canned
1 cucumber, peeled, halved lengthwise, seeded, and diced
¼ cup diced pimientos
2 tablespoons minced fresh parsley
¼ cup fresh lemon juice
1 teaspoon minced garlic
1 teaspoon dry mustard
½ teaspoon salt
⅛ teaspoon freshly ground black pepper
½ cup olive oil
3 cups cold cooked long-grain rice
Torn mixed lettuces, for serving
Sliced ripe tomatoes, for serving

Steam the green beans over boiling water until just tender, about 5 minutes. Run under cold water to stop the cooking process and retain the color; drain well. In a large bowl, combine the three beans, the cucumber, pimientos, and parsley; set aside. In a small bowl, whisk together the lemon juice, garlic, mustard, salt, and pepper. Add the oil in a slow, steady stream, whisking constantly until emulsified and smooth. Pour the dressing over the bean mixture and toss to coat. Let stand, covered, at room temperature for 20 to 30 minutes. Drain the excess dressing from the bean mixture, add the rice, and toss to combine. Taste and adjust the seasoning, adding more dressing if desired. Serve the salad in shallow bowls lined with lettuce leaves, topped with tomato slices.

SERVES 4

Sun-Dried Tomato and Basil Rice Salad with Balsamic Vinaigrette

ᐯᐰ PIQUANT olives and the smoky-tasting sun-dried tomatoes provide a dramatic contrast to the fresh flavors of ripe tomato and fragrant basil.

¼ cup balsamic vinegar
1 teaspoon minced garlic
½ teaspoon salt
⅛ teaspoon freshly ground black pepper
½ cup extra virgin olive oil
3 cups cold cooked Texmati, Wehani, or other rice
1 large ripe tomato, seeded and chopped
¼ cup minced sun-dried tomatoes packed in olive oil
2 tablespoons chopped pitted black or green olives
1 scallion, trimmed and minced
2 tablespoons chopped fresh basil
Lettuce leaves, for serving

In a small bowl, whisk together the vinegar, garlic, salt, and pepper. Add the oil in a slow, steady stream, whisking constantly until emulsified and smooth; set aside. In a large bowl, combine the rice, tomato, sun-dried tomato, olives, scallion, and basil. Add just enough dressing to coat the salad, tossing to combine well. Taste and adjust the seasoning. To serve, line a plate or shallow bowl with lettuce leaves and mound the salad on top.

SERVES 4

RICETERA...
OTHER USES FOR RICE

RICE ISN'T JUST for food. It's used to make a number of
other products, from face powder to pet food. All parts of the
rice plant are used to make something: Rice starch is used to
make glue and as a starch for clothing; rice straw is made into
paper, baskets, mats, and hats.

CHAPTER 8

Rice Desserts

Although many of us have fond memories of Mom's comforting rice pudding, our experience with rice desserts has usually stopped there. It should come as no surprise, however, that many of the countries where rice is a staple food also have their share of luscious rice desserts.

As we traverse the globe, we find the ambrosial taste of Indian *kheer* (rice pudding with rose water, cardamom, and almonds), the sublime sweetness of Coconut Sticky Rice with Mangoes from Thailand, and a surprising dessert risotto made with arborio rice, chopped fruits, and nuts. I've also included a few variations on Mom's classic; in the interest of good health, I've significantly reduced or eliminated some of the richer ingredients of traditional rice pudding. You will find no eggs, butter, or heavy cream in these "enlightened" desserts, but they are still satisfying and delicious.

NOTE: While soy milk is listed as an ingredient in many of the recipes, you can substitute another dairy-free milk, such as almond, rice, oat, or coconut milk. You can also use cow's milk if you prefer. Either way, the desserts will be delicious. Where sugar is used, I have offered the option of using a natural sweetener. These natural sugar alternatives include barley malt, rice syrup, maple syrup, honey, pureed fruit, and Sucanat, a naturally derived cane sugar product. Choose whichever sweetener you prefer, keeping in mind that these sweeteners may produce taste and textural differences in the desserts.

INDIAN RICE PUDDING WITH CARDAMOM AND ROSE WATER

༄ FRAGRANT cardamom, rose water, and coconut milk create the sublime, almost ethereal, version of rice pudding called *kheer*. Rose water and cardamom are available in Indian markets and specialty food shops; cardamom may also be found in well-stocked supermarkets. If not using regular sugar try a mild sweetener like Sucanat rather than an assertive sweetener like honey or maple syrup, so it does not overwhelm the subtle flavors of the dessert.

3 cups cooked basmati rice
1½ cups vanilla soy milk (or other milk; see Note, page 133)
1½ cups unsweetened coconut milk
½ cup sugar (or a mild natural sweetener to taste)
¼ teaspoon ground cardamom
Pinch of salt
2 teaspoons rose water
¼ cup slivered almonds
1 tablespoon cornstarch dissolved in 1 tablespoon water

Place the rice, soy milk, coconut milk, and sugar in a saucepan, bring to a simmer over low heat, and simmer gently, stirring occasionally, for 20 minutes, or until most of the liquid is absorbed and the rice is very soft. Add the cardamom, salt, rose water, almonds, and the cornstarch mixture and simmer for 5 minutes longer or until smooth and creamy. Stir, then taste and adjust the seasoning if necessary. Serve warm or refrigerate and serve cold.

SERVES 4

I Remember Mom's
Rice Pudding

∾∾ N o guilt here—just the wholesome goodness of rice, raisins, and soy milk, flavored with vanilla and cinnamon in a health-conscious version of a favorite comfort food. Since this updated pudding starts with cooked rice, it's ready in the fraction of the time Mom's was.

1 cup golden raisins

3 cups vanilla soy milk (or other milk; see Note, page 133)

½ cup sugar (or a natural sweetener to taste)

3 cups cooked short-grain rice

1 teaspoon ground cinnamon, plus extra for sprinkling

1 teaspoon vanilla extract

Pinch of salt

1 tablespoon cornstarch dissolved in 1 tablespoon water

Place the raisins in a saucepan with enough water to cover and bring to a simmer. Cook for 3 minutes, or until plump; drain and set aside. In a large saucepan, combine the soy milk and sugar and bring almost to a boil, stirring to dissolve the sugar. Add the cooked rice, cinnamon, vanilla, and salt and simmer over medium-low heat, stirring occasionally, for 20 minutes, or until the rice is very soft and creamy. Stir in the raisins and the cornstarch mixture and simmer 5 minutes longer. Cool, cover, and refrigerate, stirring occasionally, until well chilled, at least 2 to 3 hours. Serve the rice pudding in individual dessert bowls, sprinkled with cinnamon.

SERVES 4 TO 6

COCONUT STICKY RICE
WITH MANGOES

∿ FEATURED on many Thai restaurant dessert menus, this exotic creation is a soothing finale to a spicy Asian meal. If not using sugar, I find that Sucanat works best as a sugar alternative in this recipe because it has a light flavor that does not compete with the delicate taste of the rice.

1 ½ cups Thai sticky (glutinous) rice
1 cup unsweetened coconut milk
¼ cup sugar (or Sucanat to taste)
Pinch of salt
3 ripe mangoes, peeled and sliced

Soak the rice in cold water for 1 hour, then drain. Combine the rice and 3 cups water in a large saucepan. Bring to a boil, reduce the heat to medium, and simmer, stirring frequently, for 15 minutes. Remove from the heat, cover, and allow to sit while you prepare the coconut sauce. Combine the coconut milk, sugar, and salt in a small saucepan. Bring to a boil over medium-high heat, stirring to dissolve the sugar and prevent scorching. Add the sauce to the sticky rice, stirring until well blended. Cover and allow to stand at room temperature for 20 to 30 minutes to blend the flavors. Do not refrigerate, or the rice will harden. To serve, scoop the sticky rice into individual dessert bowls and surround with slices of mango.

SERVES 4 TO 6

GINGER PEACHY RICE PUDDING

∽ A GREAT way to enjoy an abundance of ripe peaches. The refreshing bite of ginger brings out the sweetness of the fruit; for an even peachier taste, substitute peach nectar for the apple juice.

1½ cups vanilla soy milk (or other milk; see Note, page 133)
1 cup short-grain white rice
½ cup apple juice
¼ cup sugar (or a natural sweetener to taste)
1 pound ripe peaches
1 tablespoon grated fresh ginger
3 tablespoons water
½ teaspoon fresh lemon juice
Pinch of salt
Fresh mint sprigs, for garnish

Combine the soy milk, rice, apple juice, and 2 tablespoons of the sugar in a saucepan and bring to a boil. Reduce the heat to low, cover, and simmer for 30 minutes, or until the rice is soft. While the rice is cooking, peel the peaches, cut in half, and remove the pits. Cut the peaches into ½-inch dice and place in a saucepan with the remaining 2 tablespoons sugar, the ginger, water, lemon juice, and salt. Bring to a boil, then lower the heat and simmer until tender. Remove from the heat and set aside. When the rice is ready, add the peaches and stir gently to combine. Transfer to dessert dishes, cover, and refrigerate until chilled, at least 2 hours. Serve garnished with mint sprigs.

SERVES 4

BAKED BANANA RICE PUDDING

⟲ I LIKE to make baked rice pudding on a cold winter day to warm the kitchen and fill the house with an inviting aroma.

2 large ripe bananas
½ cup sugar (or a natural sweetener to taste)
1 teaspoon vanilla extract
1½ cups vanilla soy milk (or other milk; see Note, page 133)
2 cups cooked long- or short-grain white rice
Ground nutmeg to taste

Preheat the oven to 325°F. Lightly oil a 1½-quart baking dish. In a food processor, puree the bananas, sugar, vanilla, and 1 cup of the soy milk. Place the rice in the oiled baking dish and add the banana mixture. Stir in the remaining ½ cup soy milk. Place the dish in a larger baking pan and add enough hot water to come halfway up the sides of the baking dish. Bake for 45 to 50 minutes, or until set and lightly browned on top. Remove the pudding from the water bath and allow to cool slightly. Dust lightly with nutmeg. Serve warm or chilled.

SERVES 4

FRUITY DESSERT RISOTTO

∾ Two favorite comfort foods—rice pudding and risotto—combine in a unique dessert that is versatile enough for a variety of flavor combinations. For example, try substituting coconut milk for part of the liquid and mangoes for the apples.

½ cup slivered almonds
2 cups apple juice
2 cups white grape juice
1 cup water
1 tablespoon vegetable oil
1½ cups arborio rice
1 cup diced apples
1 cup chopped fresh or canned pineapple
½ cup golden raisins
1 tablespoon fresh lemon juice
½ teaspoon ground cinnamon
Pinch of salt

Toast the almonds in a medium skillet over medium heat, shaking the pan frequently, until lightly browned, about 2 minutes. Remove from the heat and set aside. In a saucepan, heat the apple juice, grape juice, and water over low heat to a simmer, and keep at a simmer. In a wide saucepan or skillet, heat the oil over medium heat. Add the rice and stir until coated with oil. Add just enough of the hot juice mixture to the rice to cover and simmer, uncovered, stirring frequently, until most of the liquid has been absorbed, about 5 minutes. Repeat with the remaining liquid, adding just enough each time to barely cover the rice and continuing to cook, stirring, until the rice is tender but still firm and the risotto is thick and creamy, about 25 minutes.

About 10 minutes before the risotto is finished, stir in the apples, pineapple, and raisins, then add the lemon juice, cinnamon, and salt. When the risotto is ready, remove from the heat, stir in the toasted almonds, and serve immediately.

SERVES 4

APPLE-PECAN STIR-FRIED RICE

↶↷ Y O U can use any combination of your favorite fruits and nuts here. To make a fruit puree to serve with the dessert, use the same fruit as in the dessert or another that complements it and process in the food processor with a splash of liquid (water, liqueur, or fruit juice) until smooth, adding a little sugar if necessary to sweeten.

1 teaspoon vegetable oil
1 cup finely chopped apples
½ cup chopped pecans
3 cups cold cooked long-grain white rice
½ cup raisins
1 teaspoon sugar (or a natural sweetener to taste)
Ground cinnamon to taste

Heat the oil in a large skillet over medium heat until hot. Add the apples and pecans and cook, stirring, until the apples soften and the pecans are fragrant, about 2 minutes. Add the rice, raisins, and sugar, stirring until heated through. Sprinkle lightly with cinnamon. Serve in bowls, topped with fruit puree, if desired.

SERVES 4

Almond-Apricot Rice Cake

∾ This moist, dense cake resembles a cheesecake but has a texture similar to bread pudding. It makes a surprising change from traditional rice puddings. The clingy texture of short-grain rice works best for this dessert.

1 cup dried apricots
½ cup golden raisins
3 cups cooked short-grain rice
1 cup unsweetened coconut milk
½ cup sugar (or a natural sweetener to taste)
1 teaspoon vanilla extract
½ cup finely ground almonds

Preheat the oven to 350°F. Lightly oil a 9-inch springform pan. Place the apricots and raisins in a heatproof bowl, add boiling water to cover, and allow to sit for 10 minutes, or until soft; drain. Chop the apricots and set the apricots and raisins aside. Place the rice in a large bowl and add the apricots and raisins, coconut milk, sugar, vanilla extract, and ¼ cup of the almonds, stirring to blend well. Transfer the mixture to the springform pan, smooth the top, and bake for 30 to 40 minutes, or until firm but still a little moist. Allow the cake to cool to room temperature in the pan, then refrigerate for several hours to firm up. To serve, carefully remove the sides of the springform pan and sprinkle the top of the cake with the remaining ground almonds. Serve cold or at room temperature.

SERVES 6

RICETERA...
MORE RICE CUSTOMS

The Indonesian rijsttafel   One of the most extravagant celebrations of rice is called the Indonesian *rijsttafel,* or rice table, so named by the Dutch. This elaborate Indonesian feast features rice as the centerpiece, served with a dozen or more dishes to complement it, such as curries, stir-fries, and satés. A colorful assortment of condiments such as chutneys and other spicy relishes, freshly grated coconut, chopped nuts, sliced cucumbers, and sliced tropical fruit are also part of the banquet.

Eight-Treasure Rice pudding   A special-occasion rice dish in China that features eight different "treasures," such as dates, nuts, and candied fruits.

Kheer   This Indian rice pudding (see page 134) may be sometimes presented to Hindu priests on religious occasions.

Rice noodles   These are eaten at New Year's and birthday celebrations in Japan; their length symbolizes long life and good fortune.

Pongal   A ceremony of thanksgiving for the rice harvest that takes place in India.

In Bali   In hopes of a good harvest, rice cakes are placed on small shrines in rice paddies as an offering to the rain gods.

Index